YOU ARE
WHAT YOU
BELIEVE

John Killinger

YOU ARE WHAT YOU BELIEVE

The Apostles' Creed for Today

Abingdon Press
Nashville

Library of Congress Cataloging-in-Publication Data

KILLINGER, JOHN
    You are what you believe: the Apostles' Creed for today / John Killinger.
        p.   cm.
    ISBN 0-687-46772-1 (alk. paper)

    1. Apostles' Creed. I. Title.
BT993.2.K55   1990
    238'.11—dc20   89-29952
                                                                    CIP

*With love
to
JOHN and CHUCK and JULI,
who gave us
the best party
we ever
had*

CONTENTS

YOU ARE
WHAT YOU
BELIEVE

YOU ARE WHAT
YOU BELIEVE

Donald Miller, the well-known minister and seminary president, tells about a woman who phoned him one Saturday night.

"Dr. Miller, what do I believe?" she asked.

"What do you mean?" Miller was not sure he had heard her correctly.

"I mean," she said, "what do I believe? You see, I've just come from a party where several people got into a discussion about their various beliefs. One woman was Jewish, and she told us what she believes as a Jew. Another was Roman Catholic, and she told us what Catholics believe. Somebody was a Christian Scientist, and he talked about what they believe. I was the only Protestant in the group, and frankly, I didn't know what to say. What *do* I believe?"

"That woman," said Miller, "must have come into the church on the *confusion* of faith, not the confession of faith."

Unfortunately, a lot of people today are suffering from confusion of faith and can't say exactly what they believe. We live in an era that has seen an explosion of secularism and a diminishing of the church and its authority in public life. The majority of persons, including most members of mainline churches, consequently are not at all certain about what they are supposed to believe, much less what they actually *do* believe.

It is easy to sympathize with such people. In a world as confused and heterogeneous as ours, it is no wonder they feel lost and bewildered. Many things have happened in the present century to shake our easy confidence in what most believers once took for granted.

Two world wars, several other major conflicts, and the great suffering that accompanied them have eroded many people's faith. Camus, the Nobel Prize-winning novelist, said that he could not believe in a God who permitted the destruction and unhappiness of millions of people, including innocent women and children. In Hemingway's novel *A Farewell to Arms,* someone asks Lieutenant Henry, who was wounded in the First World War, if he is *croyant*—that is, if he is a believer. "Only at night," he replies. In the daytime, when his mind is alert, he no longer can believe; at night, some of the old yearnings return.

The age of science and technology has made it increasingly difficult to think in terms of religious causality. Many people are inoculated with just enough understanding of the laws of physics to render them immune to the great mysteries of the universe. They take a "laboratory approach" to life and, because they cannot quantify or qualify the role of the Creator, assume that the deity was only a "God of the gaps," imagined by primitive people to explain the natural phenomena for which there were no scientific explanations.

Recent advances in medicine and communications, among others, have only further removed us from a sense of the presence of God. Wonder drugs and organ transplants have given many persons undue confidence in the power of physicians—a confidence many physicians themselves will readily admit is probably misplaced. And the development of the media, especially TV and videotape, has provided us with such a vivid world of instantaneous diversion that many people now go through life without confronting the void that surrounds their consciousness. They simply turn on the tube or put on headphones and propel themselves into some vicarious world where they can escape the necessity of existential decision making.

"Who needs God, man?" asked one twisting, gyrating young man with an oversized cassette player on his shoulder and earplugs in his ears. "This is it!"

The geometric increase of knowledge in our time, with the relativism that invariably accompanies it, also has had a destructive influence on faith. "Everything in the mind is in rat's country," says anthropologist Loren Eiseley. "It doesn't die." He means we are like pack rats, especially now that we have computers—we never destroy information. As a consequence, we are overwhelmed by databanks, by stored experiences, by all there is to see and hear and know.

I remember a distraught graduate student of history. She had made straight A's as an undergraduate and had begun her doctoral program with high promise. But one day as she sat reading in the library, she simply flipped out at the realization of all there is to learn.

"I thought I heard all the books on the shelves talking at once," she said. "It was a terrible experience. I got up and ran outside. Now I don't know if I am really cut out to be a teacher."

In a world filled with so much information, people don't know what to believe. The Hindus in India have one belief system, the natives in Zimbabwe another. One religion teaches renunciation of the world; another advocates embracing it. What should a person believe? It is no wonder college professors of religion often respect all beliefs while having none of their own.

It is difficult, in a world of such extensive knowledge, to sort things out and evaluate data. As Martin Esslin points out in *Mediations,* televising the news of atrocities on a battlefield alongside advertisements for soap and deodorants tends to flatten the atrocities, make them appear of equal value with soap or deodorants. How, in a society so filled with ideas and information and so afflicted by relativism, can the sense of God or the Holy survive?

"God used to rage at the Israelites for frequenting sacred groves," says Annie Dillard in *Teaching a Stone to Talk.* "I wish I could find one." Her point is that we have so relativized the world that we have ended by desacralizing it, by removing every hint of transcendence; pantheism, the idea that everything is inhabited by a god, has given way to "pan-atheism," the idea that nothing is holy any longer.

Confusion of faith, indeed! We admire the great modern heroes of the Christian way such as Albert Schweitzer and Mother Teresa, but we don't pretend to understand how they can be so single-minded. We personally are much more in tune with Woody Allen, who says in *Love and Death*, "If God would only speak to me—just once. If He would only cough. If I could just see a miracle. If I could see a burning bush or the seas part. Or my Uncle Sasha pick up the check."

What happens when we no longer believe anything and can't act from a center of spiritual certainty, as our forebears did? They learned the Shorter Catechism: "What is the chief end of man? . . . Man's chief end is to worship God and enjoy Him forever." They knew where life was pointed, what gave it meaning. What happens when we no longer know, when the orientation is lost? We lose our sense of direction. We are like globules of quicksilver, racing this way and that with nothing to steady or guide us.

I once heard a very convincing explanation of the importance of a belief system from a completely nonreligious source, a merchant of self-confidence selling tapes on TV. What, he asked, is the most basic thing that can be described about a person? It is the person's *behavior.* Whatever else can be said, behavior remains the most obvious. But what determines behavior? It is *feelings*, isn't it? People behave the way they do because of the way they feel. And what controls a person's feelings? It is *attitude.* A person who has an optimistic attitude will feel upbeat and happy. A pessimistic attitude, on the other hand, results in feelings that are negative and unhappy.

But there is something else, he said, that lies behind attitude. It is *belief.* Beliefs control attitudes. If people believe there is a God, and that God is working for their good, their attitudes will be more positive than if they believe everything is mechanistic and there is no moral dimension of life.

If we do not know what to believe—in other words, if our belief centers have simply collapsed from the pressures of suffering and scientific preoccupation and intellectual relativism—then we have nothing with which to control our attitudes and feelings and behavior. Our human consciousness will drift without a rudder on a vast sea of meaninglessness.

We *are* what we believe.

But wait, the salesman's explanation goes one step further. Behind behavior and feelings and attitudes and beliefs, he says, there is an even more basic determinant. It is *programming.* The human mind is like a computer. It behaves the way it is programmed. It acts on the information that is fed into it. It is what we are programmed to think that determines what we believe and, in turn, our attitudes, and so on.

We resist that idea, don't we? It paints us as too mechanical, too lacking in freedom of the will. But it is true, isn't it? Our beliefs frequently are the product of our programming, of what someone else—our parents, our friends, the government—has put into our minds.

If we live among people who believe in God, who read their Bibles and attend church and live morally accountable to their faith, then we will believe in God and try to live the same way, won't we? If we live among atheists and agnostics who say that this life is all there is, you'd better grab the brass ring while you can and not worry about tomorrow, then we will tend to believe as they believe. Even if we believed in God when we began our association with such people, that belief will be challenged and weakened by our new programming.

Two sociologists, Peter L. Berger and Thomas Luckmann, call this programming *The Social Construction of Reality.* In their book by that name, they demonstrate the manner in which all human beings tend to receive understanding of what is real and valuable in life from other human beings, especially those closest to them, rather than from their own independent experimentation and perception.

If our society believes in God, we shall probably believe in God. If the society is not particularly interested in God, then we are not likely to be very committed to thoughts of a deity.

Given a society like ours, then, which admittedly is only nominally religious and given more and more to secular, hedonistic inclinations, our programming for belief is at best rather indefinite, and we are more likely to emulate such popular idols as Madonna, Michael Jackson, Sylvester Stallone, and Donald Trump than St. Francis or Mother Teresa.

The ministers I meet feel increasingly helpless as they try to turn people to God in such a world. Our efforts are so ineffectual, they say, in the face of widespread attitudes of selfishness and apathy, programming in the media, and the culture generally, which shape beliefs not toward God but toward a cynical, self-serving life-style.

The reader may feel the same.

But fortunately, belief sometimes manifests a way to assert itself against its programming. It did so in the case of Saul of Tarsus, the highly trained Pharisee who claimed to have a remarkable encounter with the resurrected Christ on the road to Damascus and went on to become the hyperenergetic thirteenth apostle.

It did so in the case of Ignatius of Loyola, a soldier accustomed to battle and courtly love. Lying in bed with a wounded leg, he asked for a certain book to read. His attendants could not find it, so they brought him another, *The Flower of the Saints*. When he had finished it, there was a visible change in his manner. He laid aside knighthood, became an ardent follower of Christ, and eventually founded the influential Society of Jesus (the Jesuits).

Belief asserted itself against programming also in the case of Sasha Makovkin, a gifted potter I met in the summer of 1987. Sasha's granduncle, Father John Vostorgoff, was the administrator of St. Basil's Russian Orthodox Church, the great landmark on Red Square in Moscow. During the revolution that created the new Soviet state, the soldiers carried all the icons from the church and threw them onto the pavement in the square. They offered Father John a bargain. If he would walk on the icons, denouncing his faith, they would permit him to live; if not, they would shoot him. For many years, Sasha did not understand why his uncle died for his belief. Why would anyone hold belief dearer than life?

Sasha, of course, belongs to a new era, a new kind of programming. His family emigrated to China, then to Canada. Sasha moved to the United States in the 1950s during the years of the Korean conflict and was initially introduced to our culture through the beatniks and the hippies. Joining the "back to the land" movement, he went to Mendocina, California, and while teaching pottery workshops there, he met Susan. She later became his wife, and they built a rude house in the woods above the town.

When a Presbyterian minister, John Tritenbach, visited a commune to which Sasha and Susan belonged, Sasha began to read the Gospel of John. Again and again as he read, he felt confronted by the challenge to believe in Christ: "God so loved the world that he gave his only Son, that whoever believes in him should not perish" (3:16); "He who believes in him is not condemned; he who does not believe is condemned already" (3:18); "He who believes in the Son has eternal life" (3:36); "Truly, truly, I say to you, he who hears my word and believes him who sent me, has eternal life" (5:24); "If you believed Moses, you would believe me" (5:46); "I am the resurrection and the life; he who believes in me, though he die, yet shall he live, and whoever lives and believes in me shall never die" (11:25-26).

"More than *eighty* times," said Sasha. "More than eighty times it says we must *believe*. I could not get away from its insistence. At last, I had to surrender to Christ."

At last, too, Sasha understood his uncle. Some beliefs can shape one's attitudes so completely that one will even die for them.

As Sasha's attitudes began to change, so did his feelings and behavior. He began to witness to this strange power that had come into his life, and to the wonderful happiness it brought. As he led

17

pottery workshops, he talked about the greatest potter of all, the One who shapes our lives into things of beauty and durability.

Now, several years later, he talks of little else. In 1987, Sasha and Susan were given a grant to go to Japan as cultural emissaries. In 1988, he went as Artist in Residence to Princeton Theological Seminary. Everywhere, he speaks of the power of belief to change human life. His own beautiful life is his greatest witness.

There is no confusion of faith in Sasha. In a world of suffering and scientific attitudes and intellectual relativism, he goes quietly and confidently on his way, for he knows what he believes. More important, he knows *who* he believes, for the faith he has found is a deeply personal faith, one in which he believes God has addressed him and he has answered with the commitment of his life.

Sasha's programming did not prepare him for this. Like Tertullian of old, he believes in spite of the evidence, in spite of the way our society has chosen to construct its view of reality. But his belief has triumphed over his programming, and he is an example of what it means to live with the certainty of faith in an age of secularism.

THE GREATEST RISK
YOU'LL EVER TAKE

It happened at a religious education conference in Texas. A woman came up to me and, with a glint in her eye, said, "I bet you can't guess what I used to be." Because the conference was sponsored by the Disciples of Christ, I replied that maybe she was once a Methodist or a Baptist.

"No," she said, laughing. "I was a professional gambler."

"Would you believe," she continued, "that I once risked $109,000 on a single spin of the wheel? It was in Vegas. I was having the hottest streak of my career. I started at the slots, just for fun. Then I went to the tables. I won two out of every three times I played. I really had it going. By 11:30 I had run my original $5,000 up to $60,000. A little after midnight, I had $109,000. My husband wanted me to quit. I said no, I had this intuition about the next spin. I let everything ride—and lost. I was sick for days. It was the biggest risk I'd ever taken." She laughed again.

"Since then," she said, "I've taken an even bigger risk. When I heard about God's love for me, and how his only Son died on the cross for my sin, I said, 'I can't let that pass me by.' I bet everything I had on it. I stopped gambling. I said to my husband, 'Sam, don't laugh, I'm going to be a teacher down at the church.' I enrolled in the seminary, took some classes in Bible, and now I'm the head honcho—I direct the whole Christian education program!"

It was the biggest risk she'd ever taken. In fact, that is the biggest risk any of us ever take—to believe there is a God and that God loves us and that we should respond to that love with everything we are and have.

What if we're wrong? Suppose we come to the end of our lives and nothing happens—we merely lose consciousness and die. We would have made a big mistake, wouldn't we? We would have gambled and lost.

A lot of respectable people have said it isn't worth the gamble. Nietzsche said God is dead. We have killed him, he said—by "we" meaning all the great thinkers and ordinary agnostics of the nineteenth century. He maintained that the people who came after them would live in a higher age for what they had done. Freud said that God is only a father-substitute, a projection of our inner need for someone like the father we worshiped when we were infants, and we all will be better off when we get over our need. Heidegger and Sartre said we shouldn't even deal with the question of God; we have quite enough on our plates with the matter of our own humanity and mortality. The Russian cosmonauts believe Karl Marx is right, there is no God; they went into space and looked around and couldn't see God anywhere.

I cannot forbear smiling at the egoism of such pronouncements . . . or remembering the little boy I saw at the seashore. The tide was rising, threatening the sand castle he had made on the beach. As the first slithery fingers of water reached out for the base of the castle and withdrew, he ran after the retreating foam with his little shovel poised aloft.

"Don't touch my castle! I built it, and if you touch it, I will spank you!"

Surely we know now that even our most respectable sciences are established upon the foundations of mystery and faith. What was it Einstein said? "You imagine that I look back on my work with calm and satisfaction. But there is not a single concept that I am convinced will stand firm; I feel uncertain whether I am in general on the right track. I don't want to *be* right—I only want to know whether I *am* right."

Talk about a gamble—that *is* a gamble! It is a great risk to build one's entire career, and a career as distinguished as Einstein's, on a theory one cannot prove, which one knows is only speculation. If Einstein was wrong about matter and energy, and someday it is proved that he was wrong, he will go down in history as a failure, a brilliant man who built everything on a faulty premise.

It is less of a gamble, for my money, to believe in God, to accept the countless personal testimonies about God's self-revelation, to side with all those through the centuries who have said, "Yes, there is a Higher Being, a Greater Intelligence, a Creator, who has formed and is directing the processes of life." It seems to me an inconceivable immodesty, not to say effrontery, to pass through the awesome cathedrals of Europe, to confront the literally millions of theological books in the libraries of Rome and Paris and Oxford, and then say, "Those people were all wrong; there is no God." For my part, if I were an atheist, I could not imagine spending an hour in the company of G. K. Chesterton or Harry Emerson Fosdick or E. Stanley Jones or C. S. Lewis without falling on my knees to confess I was mistaken and wished to join the glorious ranks of believers!

Speaking of C. S. Lewis, who can forget that great scholar's description of the way God the Adversary closed in on him? In *Surprised by Joy*, he tells of riding up Headington Hill in Oxford on the top level of a bus, when he became aware of a "moment of wholly free choice." He realized he was holding something at bay, not letting it get close to him. He felt, he said, as if he were wearing a corset or a suit of armor. In that moment of choice, he knew he could open his armor and let this advancing something into his life, or he could keep the armor closed and fend the something away. There was no duty or threat attached to the choice. It was simply his to make. And he chose to open up, to permit whatever it was that was stalking his life to come closer.

Then in his room one night at Magdalen College, the mysterious "something" revealed itself: It was God seeking entrance to his life. He tried to hold off the invasion by granting the existence of the deity as a philosophical idea he called the Absolute Spirit. But God kept coming at him. Said Lewis:

The real terror was that if you seriously believed in even such a "God" or "Spirit" as I admitted, a wholly new situation developed. As the dry bones shook and came together in that dreadful valley of Ezekiel's, so now a philosophical theorem, cerebrally entertained, began to stir and heave and throw off its gravecloths, and stood upright and became a living presence. I was to be allowed to play at philosophy no longer. It might, as I say, still be true that my "Spirit" differed in some way from "the God of popular religion." My Adversary waived the point. It sank into utter unimportance. He would not argue about it. He only said, "I am the Lord"; "I am that I am"; "I am."

Night after night, the experience returned to Lewis, relentlessly haunting him, until finally he fell to his knees, admitted that God was God, and prayed. His whole life was different from that moment on.

Was it only an illusion that Lewis experienced? Was it only the romance of an idea he couldn't fend off?

For the rest of his life, he was happy with the confession he had made. If he was living with an illusion, it was a wonderful illusion!

I have always enjoyed something I once heard my friend Wallace Fisher say. Wally was the successful pastor of a great Lutheran church in Lancaster, Pennsylvania. He is a man's man, if there ever was one—stout, virile, with a keen-edged mind and a tongue to match. There was a man in Wally's city who considered love an illusion and so had never married. He admired Wally, but could never understand why Wally seemed so happy in his marriage.

"How can an intelligent man like you submit to such a life of illusion?" he asked.

"Why, I go to bed on a cold night and snuggle with my wife," replied Wally, "while you get between the sheets and shiver by yourself. I get up and have breakfast with my wife, while you get up and eat alone. When something is bothering me, I sit down and talk with my wife until I feel better, while you have no one to talk with. Who is really living a life of illusion?"

People who never really have believed in God to the point of letting God into their existence and becoming totally different persons can hardly be expected to understand. To them, belief seems illusory and unsophisticated; they must experience it before they can begin to think otherwise. As Peter Taylor Forsyth said in *The Person and Place of Jesus Christ*, "To look at a building like the Albert Hall, or even St. Paul's, from the outside, you would have no such impression of its vastness or grandeur as you receive from its interior. And so with Christian truth. It is really and mightily true only from within." Thus it is with belief in God. From the outside, it may appear a small and tawdry thing. But, from the inside, it is magical and overwhelming.

Actually, the Bible gives no quarter to unbelievers. The Apostle Paul, in his great theological tractate to the Romans, says there is sufficient evidence of God's existence in the world around us to remove any excuse for not believing. "Ever since the creation of the world," writes Paul, "his invisible nature, namely, his eternal power and deity, has been clearly perceived in the things that have been made" (1:20). And Jesus puts it even more forcefully in a brief parable: "The kingdom of heaven is like treasure hidden in a field, which a man found and covered up; then in his joy he goes and sells all that he has and buys that field" (Matt. 13:44). In other words, anyone who disregards the evidence of God in the world and doesn't sell everything in order to serve that evidence is a fool. It isn't those who believe in God who are following an illusion; it is those who neglect to act upon the abundant evidence that God is, and therefore should be worshiped.

I confess that I cannot for the life of me understand how people can live selfishly and aimlessly from day to day, quite apart from any apparent interest in the deity. How empty, how utterly empty and hollow their existence must be! Someone—was it Rainer Maria Rilke?—asked whether it is possible to live all one's life, and a long life at that, only to discover, quite at the end, that one has lived only on the surface of things, never touching the deepest matters, never connecting with the great Spirit who animates everything. Yes, apparently it is possible. Some people careen through life from the cradle to the grave without bowing to anything higher than their own appetites and lusts. But I for one shall never understand it. It is so callous, so insensitive. Their souls must be encased in impregnable plastic, like druggists' packets that were never meant to be opened.

Don't say it is because I'm a clergyman that I see it this way, for it is the other way around; it is because I see it this way that I became a clergyman. It is not my profession that makes me talk about God; it was talking about God that led me to my profession. I was well on my way to becoming an artist—a cartoonist or an illustrator. But the Adversary of whom C. S. Lewis spoke haunted me too, haunted me until I knew there was nothing else for me to do but become a full-time servant.

I cannot tell you how many times I have wanted to quit. I have met few ministers who didn't want to. It is no picnic, contrary to the popular viewpoint. Most people who are angry with life, and therefore with God, take it out on their minister. Some do it by frontal assault; some do it subtly, in small, insinuating ways. I place in the latter category a story told by a minister in Mississippi. A parishioner appeared at his door one evening with a sack of potatoes.

"I was sorting my potatoes," the man said, "and found they were starting to rot. I thought I ought to give you some. Here."

That is subtle, isn't it, and insinuating—the kind of thing that led F. W. Robertson, one of the greatest voices for God in the nineteenth century, to say that he would be glad when his ministry was over, for he could not bear "the degradation of being a Brighton preacher."

But not many of us quit, you see, for we really believe in the God we talk about. We believe in God so deeply, so completely, so irrevocably, that nothing—not even the caviling of the saints—is able to stop us from talking about him. It is by "the foolishness of preaching," the Scriptures say, that salvation enters the world. I can tell you that we often feel foolish when we say the things we testify to, before a world that treats them as if they were mere odious drivel. But we do not stop, for we have seen the inside of the majestic hall of faith; we have stood in it and felt our hearts stop at the beauty and the glory. And we are not about to forsake the calling God has given us to witness to others who stand yet upon the outside. We have glimpsed the treasure in the field, and we will not stop short of selling every other hope we have in the world in order to serve this one, so that we may someday hear that heavenly voice say, "Well done, good and faithful servant; you have been faithful over a few things, I will make you master over many."

Forgive my little outburst of passion. But I cannot bear for people to discount what ministers say because they are ministers, as if that is what they are expected to say, the way used-car salesmen are supposed to say complimentary things about the cars they are trying to unload. Ministers really do believe in God—so thoroughly, so unavoidably, that it is extremely difficult for them to quit the ministry and become normal human beings.

For this reason, I always look with tenderness and joy on those who have recently confessed their desire to leave their ordinary lives and enter the ranks of some special service for God, as Art Hutton did.

I met Art at a retreat for Presbyterian ministers, where he was director of the church camp. I was impressed with him from the first—a strong, friendly, good-looking man with an easy manner, and a first-rate tennis player, as I found out on the courts. Art had been head of the Convention Center in Las Vegas—a high-powered job, if ever there was one. I was curious about how he found his way from a position like that to become the director of a religious camp. One day, in a quiet conversation, he told me.

He liked that job, he said, but he also liked other parts of his life, especially as an elder in his church and as a scoutmaster. One Sunday his minister preached a sermon that deeply moved him, made him realize how much God meant to him. That night he went out in his backyard under a full moon. As he communed there with God, he asked God to show him what he wanted him to do to express his love and devotion more fully.

Shortly afterward, one of Art's children returned from a week at a Christian camp near Oakhurst, California.

25

"Dad," said the child, "I've found a job for you!" It had been announced at the camp that week that the manager was leaving and a new manager was needed.

"Why not?" Art thought. "Maybe this is what God is leading me to do." And in less than two months, he was the new camp manager.

"My mother couldn't understand it," says Art. "She didn't know why anybody would take the kind of cut in salary and benefits I took. But I'm very happy and satisfied, and I feel closer to God than ever."

Maybe this is what Jesus was talking about—selling everything for the treasure found in a field. If we really believe in God and listen to the demands of that belief, it may cause us to do some strange things.

It had that effect on the woman who lost $109,000 in Las Vegas.

It also had that effect on C. S. Lewis.

And on a lot of people who have become ministers.

And on Art Hutton, who became a camp director.

Be warned—it might have that effect on you too.

A GOD
WHO REALLY CARES

The mother of J. B. Phillips, the famous Bible translator, died of cancer while he was still a boy. She had suffered off and on for a period of ten years, and during the final summer of her life, he often sat with her to keep her company. She had become a pathetic sight, even to her family. Most of her hair had fallen out; her body had become a mere tortured lump of flesh. Her mind, once keen and active, functioned only intermittently, and much of the time she did not recognize her son.

Phillips wrote in his autobiography, *The Price of Success:*

I grew angrier and angrier that God could allow such terrifying physical and mental degradation to happen to such a wonderful woman. I gave up my religious faith utterly, for what use was prayer and talk of the love of God when I returned daily to this horrible caricature of the spritely, witty mother I had known and loved? I became, as I thought, a confirmed atheist. The problem of human suffering is, I believe, the biggest serious obstacle to faith in a God of love today. (p. 37)

He was right, of course.

The litany is familiar: If God is really our Father and cares deeply for us, and if he is Almighty and can move mountains, then why does he permit us to suffer? Why doesn't he simply stop the cancer from eating, prevent the earthquake from destroying homes, and make the deserts spring up with wheat to feed the millions of people who are starving?

Many people are like young J. B. Phillips. Unable to reconcile the picture of a God who is both loving and powerful with the occasional desperate human situation, they decide not to believe any more. Better to be atheists, with reason intact, than believers with no explanation.

It is, of course, a simplistic picture of the way the world works. Suppose God did hear our prayers and made everything right every time we asked to be relieved of some pain or problem. Then *we* would be calling all the shots, wouldn't we? It would be "God, take away the pain I'm feeling" and "God, I've planted some roses, let's have rain tomorrow" and "God, I know my brother is ninety years old, but I'm not ready to give him up," wouldn't it?

If God answered all our prayers, then who would be God? God wouldn't be God! God would be only a genie, doing magic tricks to keep us happy. We would be God, wouldn't we? We would make the decisions, call the shots, run the universe.

Jesus taught us to call God our Father, and Jesus certainly knew that God has enormous power—even the power to raise the dead—but Jesus never once, as far as we know, got hung up on this dilemma of an all-loving, all-powerful God in a world of want and suffering.

Why do you suppose that is?

Did Jesus look upon suffering differently from the way we look at it? Take that night in the garden of Gethsemane, when he saw the awful specter of the cross looming before him. He knew suffering was coming, didn't he? Terrible, humiliating, excruciating suffering.

"Father, if it be possible," he prayed, "let this cup pass from me. Nevertheless, not as I will, but as thou wilt" (Matt. 26:39).

There wasn't any "If you don't help me out, I won't believe in you any longer."

He didn't say, "I will have a real problem with credibility, after all I've done in your name, if you let this awful thing happen to me."

He said, "Not as I will, but as thou wilt."

Submission.

Obedience.

Letting God be God.

Letting the Father be Almighty.

That is a different spirit from the one we usually have, isn't it? It is a controlled spirit, a disciplined spirit, a yielded spirit. It is a spirit that understands the deep things of life and knows that being healed or fed or saved from suffering is not always the best or most necessary way.

Here is a little poem by Raymond Coffin, from his book *Poetry for Crazy Cowboys and Zen Monks.* It is called "No-Mind." Zen students will recognize that phrase as a description of the state of inner peace and discipline.

> For the first time
> in four years,
> All morning walking
> the streets for bread,
> Cold rain falling from
> the sky.
> Yet not a single yen
> fell in my bag . . .
> Today's poverty
> was perfect . . .

Do you catch the spirit of that? For four years, this man had sought the way of Zen. Now, on this wet, miserable day, though nobody had given him anything, he had found it. His poverty was perfect.

This is what believing in the Father Almighty is about. Not about being protected from suffering or loss or dying, but about being glad to be alive in the world. About loving him. About falling down in homage before his mighty power.

It is why the Apostle Paul wrote in his epistle to the Romans that "the sufferings of this present time are not worth comparing with the glory that is to be revealed to us" (8:18). "Who can separate us from the love of Christ?" he asked—from what God has been doing in our behalf.

Can trouble, pain or persecution? Can lack of clothes and food, danger to life and limb, the threat of force of arms? Indeed some of us know the truth of that ancient text:
> For thy sake we are killed all the day long;
> We were accounted as sheep for the slaughter.

No, in all these things we win an overwhelming victory through him who has proved his love for us.

I have become absolutely convinced that neither death nor life, neither messenger of Heaven nor monarch of earth, neither what happens today nor what may happen tomorrow, neither a power from on high nor a power from below, nor anything else in God's whole world has any power to separate us from the love of God in Christ Jesus our Lord! (Rom. 8:35-39 Phillips)

Do the words sound familiar, yet different from the ones you are accustomed to hearing? They are the translation of John Bertram Phillips—J. B. Phillips, the adult—Phillips, who said he was once an atheist, unable to accept his mother's suffering and death.

How do you suppose Phillips felt as he translated this magnificent passage? I imagine a smile on his face that went clear down to the bottom of his soul. He was a man now, and a disciplined Christian. He knew that things in this life don't always work out as we would like. He had learned about suffering and submission. He believed that the Father loves us and will one day prove his almighty power in the world.

It is a matter of faith.

How does the old hymn "Blessed Assurance" go?

> Perfect submission, perfect delight,
> Visions of rapture now burst on my sight;
> Angels descending bring from above
> Echoes of mercy, whispers of love.

Believing in God the Father Almighty doesn't save us from suffering and loss, any more than believing in our earthly parents can save us from suffering and loss. But believing turns suffering into an offering, an oblation we give to God. It transforms it into something rare and beautiful, the way an artist takes the clay of the earth and shapes it, and fires it into an object of loveliness.

This is why Etta is crying in the exquisite scene near the end of Theodore Dreiser's last novel, *The Bulwark*. Her father, a dear old man who has suffered greatly in life, has just died, and she is sitting alone, softly weeping. Someone who comes into the room accuses her of feeling sorry for herself.

"No," she says, "you don't understand. I'm not weeping for myself. I'm not even weeping for Father. I'm weeping for *life*." Life is filled with pain and suffering. Yet, when seen in the eternal perspective, life is beautiful.

And God the Father Almighty is involved in it—more deeply and tragically and lovingly than our finite minds can ever suspect.

The *Los Angeles Times* of August 23, 1988, carried a story almost unbearable in its pathos. It was about a man named Juan Buenrostro, who now lies silently in his bed in Tijuana, tended by his wife and his mother. Juan's family was growing and money was scarce. Several times when he needed money, he had crossed into the United States to work in the fields or wash dishes in a restaurant. Apparently he decided to slip across the border again. An American school bus was parked in front of the Tijuana Cultural Center. While the students were inside, Juan crawled under the bus and wedged his body between the frame and the differential gear. To prevent falling off, he looped his belt around the bus frame. Nobody noticed, and three hours later, the bus crossed the border into the United States.

But something went wrong. As the bus roared up Interstate 5 and the students joked and sang, some of them noticed a faint knocking under the area near the rear wheels. Some even stamped on the floor in rhythm with the knocking. Forty minutes later, when the bus pulled into the parking lot at a restaurant in Carlsbad, California, Juan fell limply to the pavement. An investigating policeman said his right arm was hanging by a shredded jacket sleeve from the bus's universal joint. He had been run over by the back wheels. It was suggested that he may even have fallen to the pavement earlier and been dragged for miles. Juan could not tell what had happened, as his injuries had left him brain-damaged and passive, with a traumatically amputated arm. Now he lies all day in his bed, staring at the ceiling. There is no money for a hospital.

Juan is a father. Not the Father Almighty, but a father. He was trying to provide for his family in a world where there is unjust distribution of wealth.

What does his situation say about the Father Almighty and *his* involvement in the world of sin and suffering? Does God care? Does God suffer when we suffer? There was a big debate about this in the early centuries of the church. It was called the Patripassian controversy. *Patripassian* means "the suffering Father." Some theologians argued that, as God is Spirit and not flesh, he is unable to experience suffering as we do. What do you think? Can you imagine, knowing what you know of life and of God, that God doesn't care or is not deeply involved in everything that happens to us?

I confess, when I read the story of Juan Buenrostro, I thought about God and Christ, and what the deity went through for our salvation. It wasn't a clear image. In fact, it was rather confused. In one sense, Juan was the Father Almighty, caring about his family. In another, he was Christ, being mangled and destroyed in the process of rescuing us. But the point of the gospel, as Paul summarized it, is that "God was in Christ reconciling the world to himself" (II Cor. 5:19 NEB). How he did that *is* confused and unclear. But I personally cannot believe he was not involved in the suffering.

Juan Buenrostro fell from the bus in Carlsbad, California. By coincidence, I happened upon a copy of a sermon preached at Princeton Seminary by a young seminarian from Carlsbad. The first anniversary of the death of his little son had been a bad day, the seminarian admitted in the sermon—a cold, blustery fall day. He tried to forget by driving to the airport to meet someone. But the beautiful autumn leaves reminded him of death, and the sign at the airport was matter of fact: TERMINAL. Everywhere he looked, he thought of his son.

Where was God in all of it, he asked. Did God care?

Then, as if sharing his own nostrum, his own benediction, he quoted from a book by Nicholas Wolterstorff, *Lament for a Son:*

How is faith to endure, O God, when you allow all this scraping and tearing on us. You have allowed rivers of blood to flow, mountains of suffering to pile up, sobs to become humanity's song—all without lifting a finger that we could see. . . . If you have not abandoned us, explain yourself.

We strain to hear. But instead of hearing an answer we catch sight of God himself scraped and torn. Through our tears we see the tears of God.

That's the sum of it, isn't it? God is the Father Almighty, but it doesn't mean he is above suffering. On the contrary, he suffers more than any of us. His suffering for us is immemorial.

For young J. B. Phillips.

For Jesus, facing the cross.

For Juan Buenrostro.

For the seminarian whose son had died.

But because he is the Father Almighty, one day there will be an end to all suffering. There will be no more tears, as the book of Revelation promises. The Father will be all in all.

And, if we only believe it now, it makes all the difference in the world.

. . . creator of heaven and earth.

THE GOD WHO CAN
MAKE YOUR LIFE NEW

One of the most tragic things that has happened to humanity in modern times is the separation of work and pleasure. This separation is part of the price of an industrial society—even more, of a technological society. Most workers, no longer in charge of what they are producing, see only a small part of the final product and therefore feel alienated from the very work that consumes so much of their lives. Resentment and rebellion are a natural reaction. "Thank God it's Friday" becomes a common expression.

In such a society, we cease to think of God as a *working* God, with things to do. If *we* were God, we imagine, we would not be working; we would be at leisure, doing something easy or recreational. God must therefore be a God of leisure, a God of calm and stillness and inactivity.

But the Bible, which is the product of an age when work was more intimately associated with the person who did it, has nothing to do with such a picture. Instead, it delights in portraying God as active, creative, imaginative, working.

In the book of Genesis, God is the One who made the world. God may have rested on the seventh day, after creating the world in six days, for creating the world required a mighty effort. But soon God is back at work again, trying to reshape a recalcitrant humanity that went awry in the Garden of Eden and reached its lowest ebb in the days of Noah, when it became necessary to send a great flood to cleanse the earth of evil.

Then God is shown with a new plan. God created a special relationship with a nation of slaves called Israel—a relationship that is supposed to result in the redemption of the world.

In the book of Jeremiah the prophet, God is pictured as a potter turning a vessel on a wheel, gently shaping it to its intended use and beauty. If the clay resists the potter's touch, becomes rebellious against the hand that shapes it, it will be broken and cast aside, and the potter will begin again (ch. 18).

God is a worker, a maker.

Why?

"Caring about our work, liking it, even loving it, seems strange when we see work only as a way to make a living," says Tarthang Tulku, a Buddhist writer, in *Chop Wood, Carry Water*. "But when we see work as the way to deepen and enrich all of our experience, each one of us can find this caring within our hearts, and awaken it in those around us, using every aspect of work to learn and grow."

In other words, work is a major form of self-expression. It is how we learn who we are, and grow by learning. It is what Abraham Maslow calls self-actualization. When we make something, we see it standing outside ourselves, and we know more about ourselves than we did. We are "companioned" by our products, by what we have made.

Think of Picasso, working day after day in his studio near the Mediterranean. He did not need to work in his later years. He was already a wealthy man, a millionaire several times over. But he loved to work because he expressed himself in his work. It was how he found joy in life. It was almost as if he were playing, not working, in the great studio cluttered with paintings and sculpture. In fact, his spirit was often playful there.

His mistress, Françoise Gilot, told about a collector who came to seek the artist's validation of a painting he had bought. Picasso, barely glancing at it, pronounced it a fake. Several months later, the man returned with another painting. Picasso told him this one too was a fake.

"Aha!" said the man. "This is the very painting you were working on the last time I was here."

Picasso was unfazed. "I often paint fakes," he said.

Think of Hemingway, writing his novels and short stories. There are two things, he said, that are important—"writing and writing well"—and to him, writing well was the most important, more important even than fishing and hunting and good food and bullfights and making love. He lived to write and understood himself in terms of his work as a writer. And when he was older and could no longer think to write well, he wanted to die, to get it all over with. So he tried to walk into the propeller of an airplane, and when that didn't work, he finally put a shotgun into his mouth and pulled the trigger.

All this is to say that *creating* is God's nature, just as we often think of judging and loving as God's nature, and God has never stopped creating. Oh, there was the seventh day, of course, and the rest after making the world. But that may have been a way of blessing the institution of the sabbath day in Jewish culture, or it may even have been a touch of Hebrew humor.

Certainly God was still working in the days of the judges and kings, to make a nation out of the inconsistent Israelites, and God was working in the time of the Exile, to bring the Jews back to their homeland and start again. God was still working in the time of Jesus and the disciples, and in the days of Paul and the early church, to construct a new Israel to replace the one that had failed.

God was still working in the Middle Ages, when whole cultures were summarized in the great cathedrals and monasteries, and in the era of the Reformation, when Christianity was revitalized all over Europe. God was still working in the time of John and Charles Wesley, when a mood of revivalism spread through Britain and the colonies, and in the days of Vatican II, when the worldwide Roman Catholic Church was shaken by new programs that still cause reverberations on every continent.

And God is still working today, for love and justice and decency, wherever the work for these qualities of life goes on, whether in the churches or in Congress or in social services or in the enlightenment of Third World nations or in the freedom to dissent, in Russia or anywhere else. God will always work, as long as there is God!

I happen to agree with Robert McCracken, a former minister at New York's Riverside Church, who wrote in *Putting Faith to Work* that he couldn't understand why people are always so quick to bad-mouth God for the evil in the world, but so slow to see the good God has produced: "The evil in the world shakes faith in God; what about the good? Why talk only about the problem of evil? Why not the problem of good? What right have we to take the good for granted and seek only an explanation of the evil? Surely what we ought to seek is an explanation of the world as a whole."

It is true there is sickness in the world, and earthquakes and war and crime and poverty.

But there are also beauty and compassion and sacrifice and humility. Don't these count for something too? Aren't these in the world because God is working here?

Do we judge an artist by the scraps under the bench or a writer by the sheets of discarded paper? There was a great brouhaha in the art world when Harvard University admitted that its several large paintings by Barnett Newman had been damaged rather severely by the sun in a room where they had been carelessly displayed. Officials of the university sheepishly stored them away for several years, then brought them out and confessed their negligence. No one blamed Newman for the spoiled paintings. In fact, some critics suggested that they were still powerful in their damaged condition—perhaps even more than before, in an eerie way.

So why should God be blamed for the evil and unhappiness in the world? We should rather remember that God is responsible for the goodness and the joy—for affecting poems and golden sunsets and deeds of mercy and moments of hope!

Jesus understood.

He said that life is like a wheat field, where scoundrels or alien forces invaded by night and sowed weeds. It is necessary for the wheat and the weeds to grow up together, lest the wheat be destroyed with the weeds. But eventually—in the Judgment—they will be separated and the weeds destroyed.

It gives God pain for his creation to be marred. No makers like their work defaced and impaired. But God is working faithfully to redeem the creation, and the book of Revelation depicts a "time beyond time," when evil will be banished forever and everything will once more be "very good," as it was in the Garden of Eden.

Jesus became God's extension, God's helper, in the struggle to remake the world. Once, when some Pharisees objected to healing an invalid man on the sabbath, he replied, "My Father is working still, and I am working" (John 5:17). When there was question about healing a blind man, he said, "We must work the works of him who sent me, while it is day; night comes, when no one can work" (John 9:4). It is a most meaningful identification.

On an old barn just outside the Cotswold village of Broadway, England, there is a somewhat faded sign that reads Bellow & Son, Makers. It does not say precisely what it is that Mr. Bellow and his son make. Perhaps they erect barns. But I am very fond of the sign, for I like its implications. It implies, first of all, that Bellow and his son are rather close; otherwise they would not be working together. And it implies that they have a certain pride in what they do together, for they style themselves makers, not merely builders or carpenters or construction workers.

We might follow their lead and speak of God and Son, Makers, for this is what our religion is about. God made the world, but it was not finished. In fact, it often has shown signs that it was getting out of hand and needed to be started over. Then God's Son, Jesus, became part of the team, and they have been working together ever since.

Jesus' message to us is that we should all become sons and daughters of God, and thus joint makers with the deity. His own interest was not in the creation in general—in reclaiming the deserts and reforesting the hillsides and keeping the streams and oceans from pollution—but in the renewal of human beings. He obviously felt that if people could be restored to their compassion and sanity, the rest of creation would readily follow suit.

As far as we know, Jesus never used a word the Buddhists are fond of—*flow*—but it is a word that describes what he intended. He wanted his followers to realign themselves with the flow of God in the world, to stop interrupting the forward progress of the Spirit, to enable what he called the kingdom of God in the hearts of all people. Later, his followers would speak of not quenching or frustrating the Spirit. It all comes down to the same thing—joining the movement to restore everything to God, who made and therefore owns all that is. And when we accede to the power of God that was moving in Christ and his disciples, we ourselves are transformed. Our lives are renewed by the very process of which we become a part.

"If any one is in Christ," says the Apostle Paul, "he is a new creation; the old has passed away, behold, the new has come. All this is from God, who through Christ reconciled us to himself and gave us the ministry of reconciliation" (II Cor. 5:17-18).

There can be no doubt about it. God's major effort in remaking what he has made is centered in us. It is not focused on the mountains and the valleys and the natural resources of the earth, or upon the winds and the rains and the earthquakes that sometimes cause havoc. It is targeted upon us and our personalities, upon us and our wills. The miracle of renewal must happen in us, not in the world around us. If this were not so, and the world around us were to be restored to its original beauty and innocence, we would be very much out of place in it. No, it is God's way now to begin with us, to make new men and women of us, and the renewal of the world will follow.

Do we doubt that such great changes can happen in us? We should look at the life of Toyohiko Kagawa, the great Japanese labor leader, who said, "It is not necessary to go far afield in search for miracles. I am myself a miracle." In *Kagawa* by William Axling, we learn that Kagawa was the illegitimate son of a profligate father and a dancing girl. Both parents died when Kagawa was four, and he was sent to the country to grow up in the care of his father's wife and a foster grandmother. They raised him as a virtual slave, beating and depriving him in retaliation for his father's actions.

Sent away to school, where he continued to lead a lonely, unhappy existence, he met two missionary families with whom he found welcome and love—and Christ. One of the missionaries introduced him to the Sermon on the Mount. He read and reread it. He memorized it. He knelt, and the yearning of his heart burst into a cry for help: "O God, make me like Christ!"

If there has been anyone in our century like Christ, it was Kagawa. While he studied the Bible in seminary, he rented a tiny apartment—a room, really—in the slums of Shinkawa, where he fed the poor, cared for the sick, and befriended the friendless. The slums of Shinkawa were unbearable by modern standards— filthy, diseased, overcrowded, dangerous. Soon Kagawa had two, then five, then ten people living with him in his tiny room. One had the itch, and he contracted it. One had tuberculosis, and he washed the man's clothing each day. Another was a murderer and could sleep only if Kagawa held his hand, for he believed this warded away the evil spirit of the man he had killed.

One day a beggar asked Kagawa for his shirt, saying, "You pose as a Christian; failure to give it will prove you a fraud." Kagawa gave him the shirt. The next day the man returned and demanded Kagawa's coat and trousers as well—and got them. Kagawa had nothing to wear but a woman's kimono with a flaming red lining, the gift of a sympathetic neighbor. People laughed, but he seemed not to notice, for he was trying to follow Christ.

Kagawa studied life in the slums and began to write about the relationship between poverty and disease. As his books were published, he became famous; the government often sought his help in reforming labor policies and redesigning slum areas. He continued to live simply, sharing his resources with the poor, and when he married, his wife also assumed a life of poverty and service. She too became one of the miracles of God.

Someone has said that if only there were a thousand Kagawas in the world, it would be a different place! That is true. But there *can* be a thousand Kagawas, or a thousand miracles like the one that changed Kagawa's life—if a thousand people would open themselves to God's remaking, the way Kagawa did, and if a thousand people would pray, "O God, make me like Christ!"

The promise is that if anyone is in Christ, he or she is a new creation; the old has passed away—behold, the new has come.

This is what God wants in the world. It is what God is working toward. And God will go on working toward it until the kingdoms of this world have become the kingdom of our Christ, and all things are redeemed in him.

I believe in God . . . the Maker of heaven and earth—and the Maker of men and women!

THE SIMPLEST CREED
OF ALL

Picture an old man in a jail cell. His hair is cropped short like that of a slave. His complexion, once darkly bronzed from the sun, is now pallid. His eyes are nearly blind. Yet there is an unearthly radiance about them, and a look of enthusiasm on his face. He paces his cell, excited to be dictating a letter to some friends:

I want you to know, brethren, that what has happened to me has really served to advance the gospel, so that it has become known throughout the whole praetorian guard and to all the rest that my imprisonment is for Christ; and most of the brethren have been made confident in the Lord because of my imprisonment, and are much more bold to speak the word of God without fear. (Phil. 1:12-14)

The man, of course, is the Apostle Paul. He is in prison in Rome for testifying to his faith. Eventually he will be killed. It is the only way Caesar can silence him, can prevent him from planting new churches and talking about a God named Jesus.

What Caesar doesn't understand is that in people like Paul, persecution only fans the flames of belief. "The blood of the martyrs," as one early Christian declared, "is the seed of the church."

Paul tells his friends to live simply and humbly, to encourage love and unity among themselves. The model for this, he says, is Christ Jesus himself.

Then, at the mention of Christ, his mind is off and running. Christ is his favorite subject. Even though Christ was God, says Paul, he emptied himself and became like a servant. He was so thoroughly humbled, in fact, that he died like any other man, even on a cross.

"Therefore," declares Paul, pacing his cell like a bear, "God has highly exalted him and bestowed on him the name which is above every name, that at the name of Jesus every knee should bow, in heaven and on earth and under the earth, and every tongue confess that Jesus Christ is Lord, to the glory of God the Father" (Phil. 2:9-11).

JESUS CHRIST IS LORD!

That is where the whole faith came together for those early Christians. They had their debates about other things, the way we do. But this was the one overwhelming fact of their lives, the transforming center of their total experience—that Jesus Christ is Lord. Let the churches debate the nature of the incarnation, let them discuss the Trinity, let them fuss about methods of baptism and serving the Lord's Supper, let them quarrel over which holy writings to canonize and how to set up their local administration. There was one undebatable proposition at the heart of everything they believed—that Jesus of Nazareth was somehow the Son of God and therefore the mighty Lord of their lives!

It was the simplest creed imaginable—the creed before there were any other creeds.

How was Jesus the Son of God? That is not easy to say; the mind boggles. "He who has seen me," he said, "has seen the Father" (John 14:9). In what way have we seen the Father in him?

For many years, my father was an agricultural agent. He was very keen on soil samples. When he went out to visit a farmer and the farmer said he was not getting a good yield from his corn planting, my father would take a scoop of earth from the field, put it in a container, and mail it to the analysts at the university's school of agriculture. A few days later, he would return to the farmer and tell him the report was in.

"Your soil is too acid," he would say, or "Your soil is lacking in potash." The farmer would add the prescribed chemicals, and his crop yield would increase dramatically.

The little vial of soil my father collected from the field never told the whole story of the field. It didn't describe the old cedar posts that stood at its perimeter, or the wire nailed to the posts. It never pictured the woods on two sides of the field, or the honeysuckle that grew on part of the fence and perfumed the air in the late springtime. It didn't speak of the black crows that flew over the field, cawing and cackling at their mastery of space, sometimes landing and balancing on the cornstalks, like gymnasts in shiny black sweatsuits. But it did give an accurate reading of the content of the soil, the ingredients present to make it the kind of soil it was.

In the same way, Jesus did not tell us all that could be told about God, for there is much about God that our human minds could not comprehend. That must wait until our intelligence has been refined and transformed by death. Yet he did reveal to us the most important things we presently need to know—that God is a loving Father who seeks the restoration of all the wayward children, that God will pardon and redeem us into a life of gentle, peaceful productivity in the world if we will allow it.

When we read the four Gospels, it is like seeing a slide show of the Father; every act, every encounter, every saying is part of the profile of God, so that when we have seen it all, we know quite enough to live here on earth. And when we die and are conducted into the world of the spirit, we shall look upon the face of God and say, "I am not at all surprised, for I have already seen you in what I know about your Son."

The early Christians were excited beyond all description by this revelation of God in Jesus Christ. Again and again, the gospel story rings with the climax of the discovery and with somebody falling down to worship Jesus. Matthew's Gospel reaches its natural peak in the sixteenth chapter, when, after months of traveling together, Jesus asks the disciples, "Who do men say that the Son of man is?"

Recalling the gossip they have heard, they reply, "Some say John the Baptist, others say Elijah, and others Jeremiah or one of the prophets."

Jesus asks, "But who do you say that I am?"

"You are the Christ," says Peter, "the Son of the living God" (16:14-16). One can almost hear the bells pealing in heaven!

In John's Gospel, the climax comes nearer the end, after Jesus has been crucified and has appeared to Mary in the garden. The disciples too have seen him—all except Thomas. And then Jesus comes to the room where they are gathered, and Thomas is there. Thomas has said he would not believe, even if he could see the nail prints in Jesus' hands and feel the wound in his side.

Jesus says softly, "Here, Thomas, come closer. Put your hand here." And Thomas falls down at once, like a man stricken.

"My Lord and my God!" he says (20:28).

One day, says Paul, writing from his prison cell, everyone will bow to Jesus and every tongue will confess that he is the Lord, to the glory of the Father who sent him.

What does it mean when I confess that Jesus Christ is God's Son and the Lord of all? In the most personal terms possible, it means that he is the absolute ruler of my life, that he is now the center of everything to me, and I am no longer the master of my own destiny.

I have often expressed my amazement at what a man once said to me. I was called to his home on a Sunday morning. He and his wife had been fighting all night. His wife had received proof of his infidelity, and she had resolved to leave him. He was crying and said he did not want her to go.

"What can I do?" he pleaded.

I said, "There is only one thing you can do. You have tried to reform yourself, and that has not worked. You have been to counselors, and they have been unable to help you. Your only hope is to give yourself to Jesus Christ and be transformed into a new person."

"Oh, I can do that," he asserted. "I believe that Jesus is a very useful tool for situations like this."

"No," I said, "you don't understand. Jesus is not anybody's tool. Jesus is Lord. Nobody 'uses' Jesus. He uses us."

Later we prayed, and the man did turn his life over to Jesus. Then the three of us prayed together, and they both turned their home and marriage over to him.

A year later I was in the community again, and saw the two of them in church with their children. They were radiantly happy.

"We still have to struggle," said the wife, "but things have been *so* different."

When we confess that Jesus Christ is Lord, it means that he is our master. We don't use him. He uses us. He becomes the Way, the Truth, and the Life for us. Then we get up every morning and ask, "What do you want me to do today?"

There is no telling where we will be led when we let Christ be Lord of our lives. We go different ways because we are different people with different backgrounds and different abilities. But you can be sure it will lead somewhere.

I once heard Cliff Richards, the popular singer, tell that he had said Yes to Jesus and now finds himself speaking for Christ at churches and rallies everywhere. A man who operates a large Christian travel agency said his future began when he opened his heart to Christ. A surgeon who manages a small clinic in Zaire, treating natives who have virtually no money, said he was an ordinary doctor with a suburban home in the United States when Christ became Lord of his life and led him to Africa.

Sometimes it's dramatic, and sometimes it isn't. But you can be sure your life will change when Christ is your Lord.

Here are the words of Leslie Weatherhead, author of *The Christian Agnostic:*

It is with a sense of deep humility and reverence, almost of awe, that I, having recently passed my seventieth birthday, sit down in this quiet study, within sight and sound of the sea, to write about the Person who has meant more to me than any other for over sixty years. As a child of nine I made my little act of dedication to him all alone on January 3, 1903, and determined to serve him for the rest of my life. I remember writing down the fact in red ink in a new diary someone had given me. Needless to say, I have gone back on him since then a thousand times, but always he has held my heart in thrall and I have known no peace outside his will and no joy to compare with the experience which I sincerely believe to be due to communion with him.

One can imagine that great man, who meant so much to so many during the blitz in London, reviewing his own commitment to Christ as he wrote, then stopping for tea, a new fire blazing up where the embers of his life had been. We never get over the need for periodic reviews and recommitment, however long we live. They are part of what it means to be in Christ and to pursue the process of individuation that leads to a wholeness in which we and Christ are one.

In Peter O'Connor's *Understanding the Mid-Life Crisis*, I recently read these words from Marie-Louise von Franz: "The experience of the Self brings a feeling of standing on solid ground inside oneself, on a patch of inner eternity which even physical death cannot touch."

Paul would have agreed with that. He stood on "a patch of inner eternity" which physical death could not touch. But for him, it was entirely tied up with knowing Jesus Christ as his Lord. "For me to live is Christ," he wrote his friends, "and to die is gain" (Phil. 1:21). His very self-identity was entwined with the lordship of Christ—so much so that death itself could be only profitable, because it would bring him even closer to his Master.

My own experience confirms all this. There is no greater happiness than to be in Christ, to have one's self thoroughly interwoven with him. If I ever have any regrets about my life, it will be because I have not followed him more closely or served him more faithfully.

I remember a marvelous scene in the Stephen Sondheim

musical *Follies*. Some middle-aged people were being accused by some younger persons who represented the adolescents the older ones had once been: "What have you done with the lives we began? Why weren't you faithful to what we started?" I went back to the hotel that evening, wondering if the young man I had been would say to me now: "Why haven't you followed Christ the way I wanted you to?"

In the end, recognizing Christ as Lord comes down to one thing. It means dying to self, in order that Christ may live in us. It means giving up our liberty, in order that Christ may be free in the world. It means selling all, in order that Christ may have everything. It means being crucified with Christ, as Paul put it, so that it is no longer we who live, but Christ who lives in us (Gal. 2:20).

It sounds dreary, but it is not.

It is the richest life in the world.

It is the life for which we all were created.

Kagawa, such a faithful follower, and such a poor man all his life, wrote: "Both Mount Fuji and the Japanese Alps are but wrinkles on my brow. The Atlantic and the Pacific are my robes. The earth forms a part of my footstool. I hold the solar system in the palm of my hand. I scatter millions of stars across the heavens. The whole creation is mine. God threw it in when He gave me Christ."

Anyone who has ever really known Christ would agree. When we die to the world for him, the world is given to us. Not in terms of wealth or power or the objects many people strive for—that is not how the world comes back to us. The world comes to us in terms of inner peace and satisfaction, of joy and certainty in the plans of God, which make us one, not only with Christ but with all truth and beauty and goodness.

I have seen it happen in hundreds of people. I know it is true.

I also recognize the truth of a benediction I heard from the lips of a young minister in Mississippi:

Jesus came into the world singing;
Jesus lived singing;
Jesus died singing.
Jesus rose up in silence.
If the song is to continue,
   it is up to us.
Go in joy and peace.
Amen.

... who was conceived by the Holy Spirit,
born of the Virgin Mary, suffered under Pontius Pilate,
was crucified, died, and was buried ...

THE SCANDAL OF
OUR FAITH

I want you to recall a moment of supreme helplessness in your life—a time when you felt as powerless as it would be possible to feel.

Perhaps you had just received the news that you had some terrible, inoperable disease.

Or your car went out of control on an icy road, skidding horrifyingly toward a tree or a steep embankment.

Or you were in a foreign country and someone stole all your money and papers.

Or you were accused of a crime and had no real proof that you did not commit it.

Or someone you loved walked out on you, leaving you alone and miserable.

Human life is like that, isn't it? It is marked by moments of abject helplessness and personal anguish.

When my mother died, my father stood over her in disbelief, slapping her face in an effort to revive her. He wanted her to get out of bed and walk across the room. Raised on a farm, he remembered that sick animals often recover if they can be raised to their feet and forced to walk. She did not respond, and I am sure the poor man had never felt more helpless in his life.

I recently read Betsy White's wonderful book *Smoke Screen*, about the years of anguish her family endured when her young son became an alcoholic and drug addict. Again and again, the family thought the boy had conquered his problem and things would be better, but each time they became worse. The awful part, said Betsy, was the terrible sense of helplessness. As much as she and her husband loved their son, there seemed to be nothing they could do to stop the destruction he was heaping upon himself and the rest of the family. As often as they tried, they simply could not find a solution.

You know what I am saying.

There are times when powerlessness is the very essence of our humanity—when there is absolutely nothing we can do, and we feel like mere insects caught on the end of a pin, unable to free ourselves. We know we are incapable of halting the rot of urban centers, or stopping the progress of cancer in a friend's body, or making everybody in our family get along with everybody else, or turning our country into a nation of truth and justice, or making the future safe for our children. The saliva in our throats turns to dust, and we feel like crying out with the psalmist:

> I am poured out like water,
>   and all my bones are out of joint;
> my heart is like wax,
>   it is melted within my breast;
> my strength is dried up like a potsherd,
>   and my tongue cleaves to my jaws;
>   thou dost lay me in the dust of death.
> Psalm 22:14-15

It is here, at the very lowest point of our self-esteem, that we can best understand the meaning of the incarnation—that Christ became like us and joined us in our predicament. Although he was God, says Paul, and existed before the miraculous birth at Bethlehem, he "emptied" himself and became a human being like ourselves. He even became like a servant or a slave, says Paul—not a ruler, but a menial!

This is basically what the Apostles' Creed means when it says that Jesus was "conceived by the Holy Spirit, born of the Virgin

Mary, suffered under Pontius Pilate, was crucified, died, and was buried." This entire grouping of phrases has one purpose—to indicate the humanity of Jesus: He was conceived, born, suffered, and died. It says that Jesus, who came into the world by an unusual mating of the divine and the human, *suffered without power* under the Roman governor, who had him executed on a cross. "The death he died," as J. B. Phillips translates Paul's letter to the Philippians, "was the death of a common criminal" (2:8*b*).

I hope you will think about what this means.

It means that God joins us, not at the point of our greatest strength, where we are righteous and powerful, but at the point of our most abysmal weakness, where we can do and expect nothing. God comes to us, not where we are most godlike, living beyond our normal means and achieving transcendence by our own powers, but where we are least godlike, where we grovel in limitations and helplessness.

If we needed more proof, there is the psalm we quoted above about being "poured out like water," with all one's bones "out of joint." Perhaps the beginning of the psalm is more familiar: "My God, my God, why hast thou forsaken me?" (Ps. 22:1). It is the very psalm Jesus quoted on the cross, the famous Cry of Dereliction. In the hour of his death, which has become one of the holiest moments in Christian recollection, he identified fully and completely with our total helplessness, our inability to conquer our own suffering.

Paul, the earliest theologian of the Christian movement, called this the scandal of our faith. That the great Word of God should be invested in a humble man like Jesus, who then died on a cross, he said, was a scandal to Jews and utter foolishness to Gentiles (I Cor. 1:23).

We can imagine the experiences in evangelism that lay behind this comment:

Paul: "Believe on the Lord Jesus Christ, and be saved."
Audience: "You mean that poor fellow who died on a cross among thieves?"

53

Paul: "Yes. *That* Jesus."

Audience: "You must be kidding. God would never work for our salvation through a fellow like that. Why, the very fact that he was not saved from the cross is a sign that he was abandoned by God."

Or again:

Paul: "Jesus, who died on the cross, is the Savior of the world."

Audience: "Surely you're jesting. God is the most powerful being in the universe. How can you say that a man who suffered humiliation at the hands of Pilate's soldiers and then expired on a cross is his representative?"

Paul: "It happened as God intended."

Audience: "No, thank you, that's not the kind of God we believe in."

You see why Paul called it a scandal. It was a complete stumbling block to people's understanding. They thought that a God so powerful would act in a powerful way to save people. But the early church was stuck with a mystery: God intended to save the world through one who came without any power, who relinquished his power when he was born in a stable in Bethlehem.

Peter Taylor Forsyth, in *The Person and Place of Jesus Christ*, suggests several analogues for the self-imposed weakness of Christ. One is about a splendid young concert violinist in Russia who pities his people for their slavery and poverty. Although he knows the personal price he will pay, he identifies with a revolutionary group that presses for human freedom. He is sent to Siberia. For the rest of his life, he is condemned to perform menial labor and is never again allowed to touch a violin.

Another analogue concerns a brilliant young philosopher at a university. His father dies, leaving their vast estates without a manager. The young man must choose between his career and returning home to manage the estates, thereby saving the livelihoods of thousands of people who work there. He turns his back on the university, where all his hope and joy lie, and enters a life he finds onerous and exacting. For the sake of his father's servants, he gives up everything he counts dear and spends the rest of his days in psychological exile.

The question is, How does God think, and how would God behave? To our human way of thinking, the only logical thing would be for a God of vast power to redeem the world through an act of power and might, to change humanity by fiat, or at the very least, destroy everyone who does not measure up to the divine requirements. But God is God, said Paul, and God can turn the wisdom of this world into foolishness and the foolishness of this world into wisdom—which is what he did in Christ. We are saved, not by an act of power but by an act of weakness—by one who gave up everything and died on a cross.

Now, after all these years, there are many people who still cannot see the wisdom of God's way. Because Jesus was an itinerant rabbi who lived in a small country thousands of miles away and died cruelly as the victim of prejudice and injustice, they dismiss him as a good man who came to an unfortunate end. They don't think about it much, but if they had to imagine what a real redeemer would look like, it would probably be a transcendent guru of such power and splendor that he or she would immediately capture the world's press, and kings and queens and presidents would bow down in awe. Then these modern skeptics might begin to believe.

But the point of the gospel is that God came among us silently and unobtrusively, in a baby born in Bethlehem and raised in the hills of Galilee. In his great compassion, he touched the lives of hundreds of poor, helpless people during a brief time of ministry. Then, in an unexpected end for the divine Messiah, submitting to the growing political pressure for his extermination, he suffered under Pontius Pilate, died on a criminal's cross, and was buried in a borrowed tomb. It takes *faith* to believe that, and it is faith that converts our lives, that begins to work inside us and transform us into the souls God is preparing for the Kingdom.

When do we best understand this? Not when we are strong and everything is going well, when we hold all the high cards and life is smiling on us. But when we are down and out, when everything has gone wrong and we are so bent out of shape we don't think we'll ever bend back again, when our sense of self-esteem has been run over by an eighteen-wheeler and we are lying in the road, hemorrhaging in a dozen places—then we know what it means to have a God who emptied himself and came among us as a slave, a God who put aside all his power and joined us in our weakness, a God who can say, "I know what it feels like, for I have been there myself."

Oh, we'd like to have God reach down and save us with power when we are down and out. We become impatient when we aren't rescued after a few prayers, and sometimes we risk a complaint: "Maybe I was wrong, and there isn't a God after all." But then we settle down and realize it is better the way it is, that God is wiser than we are. We grow a little inside, and we see that getting on top again isn't all that matters, that what really matters is being at one with the God of the universe; and the God of the universe has made us one with him by coming among us in our very own weakness.

It isn't that God doesn't have power. The story of the resurrection is one of sheer power, of such energy that only an Einstein of the spirit is capable of comprehending it. But the mystery of the faith is about God's laying power aside and joining us at the heart of our humanity, with all its finitude and powerlessness. And because God has done this, no child who suffers from hunger or injustice, no adult who endures brokenness or rejection, suffers or endures alone. God is with us—in everything.

A friend of mine, a veteran of the Korean conflict, tells about a sergeant who fell in love with the children of Korea. His heart was moved by the tragedy he saw in that war-torn land—countless children running through the streets, rummaging through garbage piles, begging for a few coins. When the war was over, he and his wife adopted two Korean orphans and brought them to their small town in Ohio. But even that was not enough, and finally they and the two children returned to Korea, rented an old house that had been partially destroyed by shelling, and repaired it. They adopted Korean ways—wore Korean clothing and cooked Korean foods. Every day, the man went through the streets of Seoul and brought home another child or two, until the old house was fairly bursting with children. It was not an official orphanage; he was afraid to ask for permission to do what they were doing, lest it be denied. My friend said that twenty-four children lived in that house at the time of its greatest occupancy.

One of the children became ill with a kidney disease. The sergeant took him to Japan, where diagnosis indicated that the kidneys could not be saved. The sergeant volunteered one of his own kidneys, and incredibly, the doctors discovered there was sufficient compatibility to warrant a transplant. The operation was completed, but the sergeant developed an infection and, after a few weeks, died. The child recovered and returned to Seoul to live a normal life, and the sergeant's wife remained in Korea for sixteen more years. When she finally returned to the States, she left behind a family of more than two hundred young people.

That is what our faith says God did for us. He came as one of us—adopted our ways and lived as we live. With infinite compassion, he suffered for all humanity. In the end, he gave his life that we might have life eternal. It is as simple as that—and as hard to understand with everyday logic.

Think about it the next time you feel helpless; and remember that God has been helpless too.

. . . he descended to the dead.

WHEN LIFE
IS AT ITS WORST

The Reverend G. A. Studdert-Kennedy, one of the most popular ministers Great Britain ever produced, said more than sixty years ago, in *I Believe: Sermons on the Apostles' Creed:*

I have met a good few honest men and women who are out for reality in religion, who have said to me that if the two statements, "Born of the Virgin Mary" and "He descended into Hell" could be omitted, the short Creed of Christendom would be to them a complete and inspiring symbol of the great unseen reality for which their spirits crave; but these two statements bother them, and on the whole they would rather have left them out.

In my own experience, now half a century later, Studdert-Kennedy's observation still holds true: It is the virginity of Mary and the descent into hell that trouble believers or would-be believers more than anything else, even the resurrection of the dead and the life everlasting.

We have already dealt with the phrase "born of the Virgin Mary," indicating that for those who wrote the creed, Mary's virginity was not really the focus of that particular part. Their interest was concentrated instead on the earthly life of Jesus—that he was born, suffered, was crucified and buried. The reference to conception by the Holy Spirit and birth from a virgin was incidental—part of the lore that surrounded Jesus' origin, which they probably used for purposes of specificity, not as items of emphasis. If people today have difficulty accepting the state of Mary's sexual innocence, it surely is not essential to the more salient matters of the creed, the belief in God, Son, Spirit, church, communion of saints, forgiveness of sins, and resurrection of the body.

Now let us examine the business of the descent into hell and see what we can make of that.

To begin, let us make a clean breast of things by saying that early Christians obviously did not think it a matter to make much fuss over either. As William Barclay points out in *The Plain Man Looks at the Apostles' Creed,* it was not a part of the baptismal confession of the Church of Rome, which was the model upon which the Apostles' Creed was based; and Rufinus, writing about A.D.400, noted that it was not included in the earliest version of the creed itself. Moreover, the creedal statements of three great church fathers—Ignatius, Irenaeus, and Tertullian—contain no reference to it, nor does the Nicene Creed, the other great creed still in use in Christendom. Its first known use in a creedal document was in the so-called Symbol of Sirmium, about A.D.360, and it first appeared in the Apostles' Creed in A.D.570, more than half a millennium after the death of Christ.

Why was this? Perhaps it was because "he descended into hell" was, in its true meaning, a redundancy, merely reemphasizing that Jesus had truly died. The original reference, you see, was not to hell at all, but to Hades, the place of death.

Modern translators, who understand the ancient references better than did their medieval and Reformation-age counterparts, have shown us that the New Testament makes a careful distinction between these two concepts. *Hell* is a place or state of punishment, while *Hades* is simply the grave, or the state of being dead. The Hebrew word for Hades is *sheol*, literally translated "the grave." Like the underworld of Greek religion, it was imagined as a dull, colorless place, where souls led a shadowy existence without hope of escape. Hell, on the other hand, was thought to be a place of extreme torment, where souls suffered much more than in Hades.

An example of the confusion that once occurred in translating the two concepts is shown in Acts 2:27, a quotation of Psalm 16:10. The Authorized, or King James, version of the scriptures says, "Thou wilt not leave my soul in hell." But both the Revised Standard Version and the New English Bible translate correctly, "Thou wilt not abandon my soul to Hades." James Moffatt, the Scottish translator, simply used the word "grave."

Because Christians in earlier centuries were not aware of the distinction, a very imaginative tradition developed which pictured Christ as descending into hell, the region of torment, and leading out the souls of people who had been condemned there in previous generations. The tradition is embodied, for instance, in *Storie della Vita di Cristo,* a remarkable series of cartoon-like paintings by the fifteenth-century artist Baldovinetti, in the Museum of San Marcos in Florence. In the painting that follows his burial, Christ is shown standing on the gate of hell, which has been knocked off its hinges. Under the gate lies the writhing Devil, while crowds of people stream through the gateway. This was known in the Middle Ages as "the harrowing of hell"— Christ's assault on the place of punishment to liberate all the captive souls.

Now, in a more enlightened and less literalistic age, we see the original intent of the creed—that Jesus descended not into hell but into the grave, into *sheol,* the world of death and shadows. Those who inserted the phrase about descending into Hades were merely attempting to reinforce the fact that Jesus was dead. In a phrase I often heard as a boy, he was *dead as a doornail,* totally and completely dead.

Instead of saying, "He descended into hell," we could well say, "He lay in a state of death." The newer version of the creed handles this well: "He descended to the dead."

From a pastoral point of view, this should have great meaning for us, especially at those awful times when someone we know lies cold and still in death. What a terrible experience it is to have a loved one in this condition. When do we ever feel more helpless? When does mortality ever seem a greater curse? A mortician once told me that the worst moment in his business is the moment he first admits the family into the viewing room to be alone with the corpse of a loved one.

"People are invariably stunned," he said. "They do not know how to cope with a body from which life has gone."

In my own experience, I would say that if there is a worse moment, it is when families say good-bye to a corpse before it is cremated or interred. I was once a pastor in a small town in New England, where it was the practice for each family member to say a personal good-bye to the body before it left the funeral chapel. Often, people kissed the bloodless face or lips of the body. They could not bear to have the coffin closed and never again see that familiar face.

It is probable that people today have more difficulty handling the experience of death than did people of earlier generations. We are less exposed to bodies and death. In their time, it was common for grieving families to prepare the corpses for burial and hold wakes in their homes. The bodies of loved ones would lie in state in the parlor or living room, and friends would call to pay their respects, sometimes sitting in the room for hours.

I have vivid recollections of a wake I inadvertently attended years ago when I was a freshman at Baylor University. On Friday evenings, I assisted at a mission in the riverfront area of Waco, Texas, where the migrant farm workers swarmed into the bars at the end of the week. One night a friend called me over to meet a wretched looking fellow named Leroy, who was sitting on the curb. Leroy said he was the son of a minister. His father had died the day before and, although he was not a drinking man, he had come to drown his sorrows in booze. Now he was repentant and wanted to return home, where his father's wake was being held. But he did not wish to go alone. Would my friend and I accompany him?

Gallantly, we agreed and began to follow him. A soft rain was falling as we passed the sign that marked the city limits. Suddenly the pavement stopped, and we were walking through pitch blackness in soft, velvety mud. I began to fear we were being set up for a mugging. But soon we saw some lights in the distance and came to a small shantytown. When we arrived at Leroy's house, fifteen or twenty men were sitting on the front porch under a naked light bulb. Inside, in the living room, an equal number of women were ranged around the room, flanking a coffin set against the wall. Leroy fell on his knees before the body of the elderly man in the coffin and began to cry. The women went on talking, as if we were not there.

Presently Leroy wiped his eyes and arose. He confessed that he had spent all his money, but would like very much to purchase some flowers for his father. Could we let him have a few dollars? I gave him the two dollars I had in my pocket, and my friend also gave him a dollar or two. As my friend knelt there with his arm around Leroy, I went out on the porch.

"Look after Leroy, will you?" I asked one older gentleman. "He's pretty broken up about his father's death."

The dark wrinkled face regarded me a moment. A wide smile revealed a patchwork of gold and ivory.

"Did he tell you that was he daddy?" asked the man. "That ain't he daddy. He daddy live up in Oklahoma!"

I didn't tell my friend. He felt too good about what we had done. And I suppose I figured the experience was worth a couple of dollars. It was my first wake.

Whoever the elderly man was, he was very dead. He did not move. He merely lay there, cold and lifeless.

This is the point of the New Testament witness to Jesus' death. He was totally, completely dead. There was no life left when he was taken down from the cross. He had descended into Hades, the land of whispers and shadows, where all the dead go.

The poet Nietzsche is reported to have cried out, as his eyes closed in death, "Good-bye, sun! Good-bye, sun!"

Hades is a place of darkness.

The existentialist writers—Heidegger, Sartre, Camus, and

others—have reminded us of the importance of living with our mortality in mind. Of all living things, says Heidegger, only human beings have *das Sein zum Tode*, "the being [that exists] toward death." We alone are able to contemplate our nonexistence, our ceasing to be alive in the world. The very contemplation shapes our lives. It permits us to decide how we shall live in the time we have left—even to write our own epitaphs.

One of Ingmar Bergman's films, *Wild Strawberries*, opens with a scene in which a man is watching a funeral cortege. As the old-fashioned, horse-drawn funeral carriage turns a corner, a wheel runs upon the curb, the casket is tipped out into the street, and the body rolls out. The cortege proceeds as if nothing has happened. The viewer, horrified, approaches the body, intending to lift it back into the box. When he turns the body over, the face on the corpse is his own!

The man's whole life is changed because of this experience.

This is what the existentialists mean. We *choose* what we shall be, how we shall live, regardless of our circumstances. And because we have the power to choose, it is good to be reminded of the barrenness of death, when life is at its absolute worst because it is spent and gone.

I said that the death of Jesus has pastoral meaning.

It does.

Jesus was dead in the same way our loved ones are dead, the same way we shall be dead. He fully experienced the limpness and emptiness of death that will be our lot. Those who grieved for him beheld nothing more than a corpse. His eyes were unseeing, his ears unhearing. The strong heart that once had pumped blood lay still. The hands that once had healed the sick lay inert and lifeless.

He was as dead as dead could be—a totally lifeless corpse.

We must believe he was dead before we can believe *that he rose again*—which is the heart and center of our Christian faith.

On the third day he rose again . . .

THE ASTOUNDING EVENT
AT THE HEART OF FAITH

In the Courtauld Gallery in London hangs the painting titled *The Incredulity of St. Thomas* by Michelangelo Caravaggio. It depicts the scene in the upper room when the risen Christ appeared to the disciples. Thomas, the one known as the doubter, is stretching forth his hand to touch the wound in Christ's side. He cannot believe his Lord is alive again.

And well he can't!

We would all have a similar problem.

I think of my father's death—the call that came; the long drive to get there; the funeral home where his body lay. He looked better in death than he had in life. We shed some tears and stood there for hours as friends came to pay their respects. We went to his room in the nursing home where he had lived the last years of his life and took his clothes from the drawers and the closet. The room seemed strangely empty without his presence. We had his graveside service on a sunny morning that turned suddenly cold and blustery as we said the words of the prayers. In the afternoon I returned to the cemetery and stood by the freshly filled grave. Nothing would have surprised me more than if he had come back that evening and stood in the room where we gathered to talk. Nothing would have effected a greater change in the way I look at life or the way I live from day to day. I would have been as incredulous as Thomas.

Jesus was really dead. The Gospels went to great length to make this clear. He was not in a swoon, later to revive in the tomb. He suffered and died on the cross. When the soldiers came to make sure, one of them pierced his side with a sword. Two of his followers took the body down, prepared it for burial, and placed it in a tomb, where a stone was rolled to secure the body. The body lay there from Friday evening until Sunday morning—three days, by Jewish reckoning. And then suddenly he was alive again!

The Bible is very graphic about these things. In the Gospel of John, Lazarus lay in the grave four days before Jesus' arrival. When Jesus ordered the stone removed from the tomb, Lazarus' sisters said, "Oh no, Lord, he has been dead for four days! By now his body will be offensive from decomposition!" And Jesus had been in the grave for three days, only one day less than Lazarus. His body too should have been decomposing. That is what is so amazing. Suddenly this very dead body, this decomposing body, was alive and appearing to disciples everywhere!

It is our problem today that we don't really believe it.

We *say* we believe it.

But we don't *really* believe it.

We can't.

We don't know *how* to believe it.

We only *half* believe it.

We have heard it all our lives, and so we half believe it, but we can't fully believe it, because we don't think such things actually happen. There must be some explanation we don't go into.

It's as if we had always heard about a man who walked across the Atlantic Ocean from England to New York. Common consent might enable us to agree that it once had happened, but down deep in our hearts, we couldn't actually accept it. Our experience tells us that people can't walk across the ocean. Neither do they rise from the dead.

We are simply stuck with a gigantic absurdity at the heart of our faith—an act so audacious and incredible that believing it would stand all our other belief systems on their heads. So we come to church and pretend to believe that Jesus rose from the dead, and then we go out to our jobs and homes and everyday lives and remain unconvinced in our hearts.

When we are confronted by the resurrection, this enormous absurdity, we must opt for one of three possibilities:

1. It didn't happen. It is merely a fiction invented by the early church.

2. It did happen, and therefore we don't understand the world we live in as well as we thought we did.

3. It did happen, but only because there is a Power so great that it can contravene the laws of the world as we know it.

Now, from the viewpoint of those closest to Jesus, it *did* happen. There can be no doubt about that. There are three major pieces of evidence.

First, there was the empty tomb. No fewer than four followers saw the empty tomb and reported it.

Second, there were all the appearances of the risen Christ—to Mary in the garden; to two disciples on the road to Emmaus; to ten of the disciples in the upper room; to those ten again, plus Thomas; to several disciples by the Sea of Galilee; and then to more than five hundred followers at once.

Third, there was the incredible change in the attitudes and behavior of the followers. Before the crucifixion, they acted from cowardice and confusion. After the resurrection, they were transformed into pillars of courage and decisiveness, ready to die for their faith. This was no mere shifting of mood. Something had happened that altered the very nature of their beings.

I said we must opt for one of three possibilities. Perhaps I was wrong, and we can opt for two possibilities—both the second and the third. That is, it is probably true that we don't fully understand the nature of the world we live in *and* that God may well have intervened in an unusual way to rescue that beloved Son from the grave.

Let me unpack that a bit.

It is true that we don't always understand the world as well as we think we do. Today we tend to be a lot more skeptical of faith than of science, with the result that we are sometimes deluded by science and so-called scientific evidence. The truth is that much of science is still unproven and perhaps even unprovable conjecture—systems of hypotheses that hold together very well within themselves but admit of no real verification from the outside. The most outstanding physicists of our time confess that one small piece of new information, one daring bit of mathematical breakthrough, might totally alter the way we presently understand matter and space.

And what of parapsychology and all the particles of information it offers? People have real experiences—at least, they say they are real—of ESP and clairvoyance and visitation and life-after-life. How do these fit into our view of things? If we were strictly scientific, we would never accept a worldview that excludes evidence that does not fit. Real science, on the contrary, pays closest attention to the information that cannot be fitted neatly into its patterns and theories.

So we must beware of being scientific bigots, just as we must beware of being religious bigots. In a world where realities are still up for grabs, it is best not to be overly dogmatic about anything.

But suppose our environment is basically submissive to rational patterns and that, at last, we are beginning to discern what they are. Does this mean that God cannot behave as God wants, despite the laws of nature—that God cannot throw away the script and improvise in a totally divine way? After all, the very name *God* implies the freedom to do what God wants, doesn't it? Is God bound by anything? If so, then God is not God.

The followers of Jesus knew that people do not normally revive after they have died—especially after they have been dead for three days. This is why they were so surprised, so galvanized, by the resurrection. If they had expected it, it would have been otherwise. They would not have run to the tomb on the report of its being empty. They would not have been transformed into pillars of courage and decisiveness. And when it happened, when they learned that Jesus had risen from the grave, they declared immediately that *God* had done it.

"This Jesus, whom you crucified," says the substance of Peter's speech to the Jews at Pentecost, "him has God raised up and made to become the Lord and Savior of us all." There was no doubt in their minds: *God had acted in an extraordinary way to restore Christ to the world of the living.*

God is God and, whatever the nature of the world, can do anything the divine will chooses to do.

How does the old hymn go?

> I sing the almighty power of God,
>   that made the mountains rise,
> that spread the flowing seas abroad,
>   and built the lofty skies.
> I sing the wisdom that ordained
>   the sun to rule the day;
> the moon shines full at God's command,
>   and all the stars obey.

Isaac Watts wrote those words—the same Isaac Watts who wrote "When I Survey the Wondrous Cross" and "O God, Our Help in Ages Past." He knew about the power of God. He didn't doubt that God could frame the heavens or command the stars to move or raise Christ up from the tomb.

What it all comes down to is that when you say *God*, you say *miracle*. It's as simple as that.

I am thinking of what happened to a friend several years ago after she was operated on for cancer. The doctors said she was riddled by the disease and would never be well again. As she lay in her room at the hospital half dead, just wanting to get it over with, a woman appeared by her bed. She said she was sent to give a massage. The woman wore foreign clothing and a turban, unlike the nurses who regularly came into the room. As her hands moved over my friend's body, she began to feel well again. She could not believe how well she felt.

When a nurse came into the room, my friend asked about the

woman in the turban who had given her the wonderful massage. The nurse replied that there was no such person on the staff.

Much later, when my friend was speaking to a large gathering of people, she saw the woman in the turban slip into the back of the room. She smiled, but after the meeting she was gone. My friend never saw her again.

I saw my friend only a few months ago. She was beautiful. It had been more than ten years since the strange woman gave her the massage. She is convinced that the woman was an angel from God.

Who is to say she is wrong or can give another explanation?

Maybe it is a fault of ours that we become impervious to miracles in the modern world. Maybe we see so few because we don't expect to see them at all. As it is, they must crash in upon us and convince us against our will.

The resurrection of Jesus, says poet Chad Walsh in *God at Large*, is "a mind-breaker." "The cross is a heart-breaker; the empty tomb is a mind-breaker." And both our hearts and our minds need to be broken, especially if we are under any illusion that they can get along without God.

What happens when our hearts *and* our minds are broken by God?

Then we have a chance to be joyous.

Not in any little momentary way, but in a cosmic sense. The people of the resurrection are happy people. They know that God is in charge of the universe, that God will not be put off by history, that eventually all the promises of the prophets shall come to pass, and there will be "a new heaven and a new earth."

Oh, they have their sorrows. They are no more immune to suffering than other people. They may even suffer more.

But deep down they are happy, for they have seen the end of the story and know it is a comedy, not a tragedy. They know that in the end the Lord Jesus will reign over everything.

Mrs. Copeland is a good example. When I was a freshman at college, I took my meals in a wonderful old boarding house run by a plump little woman named Mrs. Copeland. She was a kindly woman who has since reminded me of Aunt Bea on the old *Andy Griffith Show*. Mrs. Copeland was one of the dearest saints of God who ever lived. Her husband had been dead for years, and she survived primarily on his railroad pension. She couldn't have made a penny on her boarding house, for she fed us lavishly and only charged eight dollars a week. She always said she did it because she loved boys and wanted to help us get through school.

Dear old Mrs. Copeland had her share of troubles. Her health was not always good, and there were always bills to be met, which she rarely had the cash to take care of. But I never saw her despair. On the contrary, I can see her now, wiping her hands in her apron, her lips trembling a little. And I can hear her saying of some momentary problem, "If our Lord Jesus could rise up from the dead, I know he will help me with any little troubles I have." Then she would go back to work, cleaning and cooking and serving as if nothing was the matter at all.

"If our Lord Jesus could rise up from the dead, I know he will help me with any little troubles I have."

That's the size of it, isn't it?

If we really believe that Jesus rose again from the dead, then we see the world differently from the way other people do. As incredible as it may seem, we know God is in charge of everything.

. . . he ascended into heaven,
is seated at the right hand of the Father,
and will come again to judge the living and the dead.

THE
UP-AND-COMING
CHRIST

Of all the articles in the Christian creed, the ascension of Jesus into heaven is one of the hardest for the modern mind to grasp. We long ago gave up the idea of a three-story universe, with heaven above, earth in the middle, and hell below. To picture Jesus, then, as a kind of Peter Pan, rising in clouds of mystery to be taken into the bosom of God the Father, is difficult at best, impossible at worst.

As William Barclay observes in *The Plain Man Looks at the Apostles' Creed*, no artist has ever succeeded in painting the scene without having it appear either grotesque or ridiculous.

The best rendering I have seen is a brass boss about three feet wide on the ceiling of York Minster in England. The artist, whoever he was, had a fine sense of humor. He depicted the soles of a pair of feet, seen from below, with the hem of a robe forming a circle around them; beyond this were the upturned faces of the Virgin Mary and eleven disciples, all looking up.

There are indeed biblical bases for the concept of the ascension. Both Mark and Luke refer to it, though the text in Mark is part of an addition which modern scholars do not accept as authentic, and the phrase in Luke—"carried up into heaven"—is also not found in the most reliable ancient manuscripts. But Luke does solidly refer to the ascension in the first chapter of the Acts of the Apostles: "As they were looking on, he was lifted up, and a cloud took him out of their sight" (1:9). Also, several references of an inferential sort are found in the Gospel of John (3:13, 6:62, 20:17) and throughout the New Testament, as in the brief creed in First Timothy 3:16:

> He was manifested in the flesh,
> vindicated in the Spirit,
>   seen by angels,
> preached among the nations,
> believed on in the world,
>   taken up in glory.

What we must understand today is that, given the primitive cosmology of the early Christians—their three-story universe—they expressed Jesus' departure in the only way that made sense to their culture, by saying he was taken up into heaven. In the Old Testament description of the departure of Elijah, the most popular prophet in the history of Israel, Elijah was carried to heaven in a chariot of fire (II Kings 2:4-12). Jesus' ascension was not that dramatic, but it achieved the same purpose—to express the idea that God had now received him into the heavenly domain.

If we were to attempt to express the same thing today, we would probably say very simply that Jesus "disappeared" and was no longer seen in the flesh by the disciples. He did of course materialize again for the Apostle Paul, who claimed to have seen him, and possibly for others, which means that he did not go very far away. And it is well known that he promised the disciples during the final meal that he would never be very far from them; again, in the so-called Great Commandment, that he would always be with them, even "to the close of the age" (Matt. 28:20).

The point of the whole matter, of course, is the *glorification* of Jesus. The humble servant who had been faithful unto death and cruelly murdered on a cross was now taken up into heaven and set down at God's right hand, the undisputed place of honor in any royal court, implying sonship and next-in-power.

Glory is something our age does not understand very well. To us, it carries overtones of the Hollywood era, as of something out of a Cecil B. DeMille movie. But in the age of the Bible it was something much different. To a certain extent, it was mirrored in the victories of Alexander the Great or Augustus Caesar, and in the fantastic court scenes of the richest kings. Yet the glory of God was conceived of as going far beyond the dreams of earthly monarchs. Where earthly streets were usually dirt or stone, the heavenly streets were paved with gold. When earthly kings were serenaded by minstrels or bands of dancers, God was encircled by angelic choirs. Though earthly courts were plunged into darkness every night, the heavenly court was constantly illumined by the divinity itself.

The early poet who completed the Lord's Prayer for oral repetition by adding the resounding phrase "for thine is the kingdom, the power, and the glory" knew what he was doing; and the doxology, a song celebrating the *doxa* or "glory" of God, was always a central part of Christian worship.

When Jesus was "taken up in glory," it was the Father's way of acknowledging their relationship and honoring his Son. The one who had been broken in earthly combat was made triumphant in the heavens, and would one day return to earth as judge of all creation.

Because a thousand years are as a day in the sight of the Lord, and God had known from the beginning how everything would be, the Son's place at his right hand had been prepared from the foundations of the world. No one else could occupy it.

When I was pastor of a church in Lynchburg, Virginia, the headquarters of television evangelist Jerry Falwell, I remember seeing in the local paper's Forum column a letter that lavished fervent praise upon the evangelist: "Why, when I get to heaven, I expect to see Jerry Falwell there, seated on the right hand of God the Father Almighty."

As much as he surely appreciated such confidence in him, I expect that Mr. Falwell winced at such a statement, since *only the Son* can sit at the Father's right hand. That place of utmost glory has been ordained for him from the beginning of time.

This means that God has set an eternal seal on *all the teachings of Jesus* and on *the example of Jesus* and on *the saving power of Jesus.* While there may be truth in all religions, there is something special in Jesus. While there may even be salvation in other religions, Jesus is the Savior of the world.

The great Christian missionary E. Stanley Jones, a close friend of Mahatma Gandhi, commented that after Gandhi's assassination, the radio constantly broadcast programs that eulogized the father of that great land. Mrs. Naidu, a well-known Hindu poet, spoke on Sunday, three days after the assassination. She had been in frequent contact with the Christian community in India, and her words carried an eloquence born of her emotion: "O Bapu, O Little Father, come back. We're orphaned without you. We're lost without you. Come back and lead us."

Jones said he could sympathize with her plea, representing the cry of a stricken nation. But as he sat there he thought, "O God, I'm grateful I don't have to cry that cry for the leader of my soul: 'O Jesus, come back. Come back. We're orphaned and stricken without you.'" He knew that his Master had been received in glory to sit at the right hand of God the Father and that he *is* coming back to redeem the entire world.

Gandhi was a great man.

But Jesus is Savior of the world, "and will come again to judge the living and the dead."

It is his glorification and place of honor in God's sight that will enable him to judge the entire world. Put to death by the sword, he shall return with a sword, dividing the just and the unjust, the good and the evil.

The New Testament is insistent upon this. It is no incidental doctrine, but one at the very heart and core of biblical faith. When the King comes, heads shall roll. When the Prince arrives, the mighty shall tremble.

In the prophecies that surround the coming of the Messiah, John the Baptist had said,

I baptize you with water for repentance, but he who is coming after me is mightier than I, whose sandals I am not worthy to carry; he will baptize you with the Holy Spirit and with fire. His winnowing fork is in his hand, and he will clear his threshing floor and gather his wheat into the granary, but the chaff he will burn with unquenchable fire. (Matt. 3:11-12)

This imagery is similar to that in Jesus' parable of the wheat and the tares. The kingdom of heaven, he said, is like a field where a farmer sowed wheat, and during the night, an enemy came and scattered the seeds of tares, or weeds. When the weeds sprang up among the wheat, the farmer's servants asked if he wanted them to dig up the weeds.

"No," said the farmer, "lest in gathering the weeds you root up the wheat along with them. Let both grow together until the harvest; and at harvest time I will tell the reapers, Gather the weeds first and bind them in bundles to be burned, but gather the wheat into my barn" (Matt. 13:29-30).

It is a cosmological picture of the way God looks upon evil. For the present, evil is allowed to grow in the world because uprooting it would mean the end of the growing time for good as well. But the moment is coming when the glorified Son of God will return for the eternal harvest, and when he does, every person, living and dead, will be called into judgment.

Visitors to the new cathedral in Coventry, England, which replaces the old one destroyed by Nazi rockets in World War Two, have seen the haunting sculpture by Clarke Fitz-Gerald, *Plumb Line and the City*. It depicts a brass plumb line and plumb bob hanging over the dark figure of the city of Coventry, like the famous vision in the ancient book of Amos.

"Amos, what do you see?" asked God.

"A plumb line," said Amos. Then God said,

> Behold, I am setting a plumb line
> in the midst of my people Israel . . .
> the high places of Isaac shall be made desolate,
> and the sanctuaries of Israel shall be laid waste,
> and I will rise against the house of Jeroboam with the
> sword. (7:8-9)

The glorified Son is the world's plumb line.

We are judged by our faithfulness to him and to his teachings.

When he returns, it will become apparent who has been good and who has been evil, who just and who unjust.

It will be a day of awful reckoning.

As the Bible says, there will be weeping and wailing and gnashing of teeth. People will cry for the rocks to fall upon them and rue the day they were born.

Peter Jan Sellars, a brilliant young producer who, for three years, was director of the Kennedy Center in Washington, D. C., discussed our contemporary culture in a television interview with Garrick Utley. Culture, he said, is supposed to guide people. It is supposed to stop them occasionally in their tracks and say, "Hey, you are missing this! You should see this! This is worth thinking about!" But our culture, he said, doesn't do this. It only makes it easier for people to glide along without thinking about things. It isn't really serving them at all.

Christ the Plumb Line says, "Stop! Your culture is often wrong. Doing what others do is not always the best way to live. You must ask, What does God want? and then, if necessary, go against your culture, risk opposing it."

According to the teachings of Christ, you see, Lee Iacocca isn't the model for modern living; Mother Teresa is. Donald Trump and Joan Collins aren't the models; Rhodes and Lois Thompson are.

Do you know Rhodes and Lois?

They are good, simple folks in Enid, Oklahoma. Rhodes is a professor at Phillips Graduate Seminary. He and Lois have never had a lot of money. They are always sparkling clean and well-groomed, but they don't spend a lot on clothes. They drive an adequate car, but rarely a new one. For the last nine years, they have been giving all their extra money to provide housing, medical care, and emergency assistance for the poor through Habitat for Humanity, Christian Medical College and Hospital in Vellore, India, and Church World Service. During this time, they have given more than $53,000 to these ministries.

When Christ returns, I would rather be like Rhodes and Lois. I know they will pass the test. They will hear the Master say, "Well done, good and faithful servants."

But our culture doesn't teach us to do this. Our culture teaches us to pamper ourselves, indulge ourselves.

Our culture is wrong.

Do you want a beautiful picture of love?

It is in a story told by Gerda Weissman Klein, who was in a German concentration camp during the days of the Holocaust. Most people, she said, think of the camps as snake pits—places of hardship where people stepped on each other to survive. But it wasn't like that at all; there was much kindness and understanding among the prisoners. Gerda had a young friend named Ilse. One day Ilse found a raspberry in the camp. She carried it all day in her pocket to present it to Gerda that night on a leaf.

"Imagine a world in which your entire possession is one raspberry," said Gerda, "and you give it to a friend."

Christ would bless such a gift. When he returns to judge the world and separate the wheat from the weeds, he will remember Ilse for her kindness and say that she did well.

In fact, he probably has adjudged her favorably already.

But in the linear time scheme of the biblical story, he is now in glory with the Father, whence he shall come again, in a great cataclysmic event, to pass judgment on the living and the dead.

With the saints of the early church, we pray *Marana tha*, "Our Lord, come!"

THE SPIRIT AND POWER
OF FAITH

"Who or what is the Holy Spirit?"

I asked this question of five persons.

"Should I know the answer to that?" answered the first.

"It's the same as the Holy Ghost, isn't it?" said the second, obviously a little uncertain.

"Sounds scary to me," said the third.

"I don't know," admitted the fourth. "I'm not into all that New Age stuff."

"It's the Spirit of God—I think," ventured the fifth.

The interesting thing is that these five people were not random pedestrians approached on some street corner of the city. They were all members of a Christian congregation encountered in the halls of their church building. Four were adults, one was a teenager. Obviously this particular church is not doing very well in teaching a fully rounded understanding of Christian theology.

Certain charismatic congregations—those emphasizing the so-called Third Person of the Trinity—would do much better. They continually talk about the Spirit. But mainline Christianity is basically confused and ignorant on one of the most vital subjects in its theological repertoire. The charismatic revival that broke out a few years ago was an inevitable response to this confusion and ignorance. Those who fostered it were merely trying to discover—or rediscover—the secrets of the power and vitality that marked Christianity in its early years.

A cameo picture of this power is found in the book of Acts, where Luke describes what happened to Jesus' followers shortly after his ascension. They had gathered, apparently to observe a major event in the Jewish liturgical calendar, the Feast of Weeks, or Pentecost. What happened is best told in Luke's own words:

> And suddenly a sound came from heaven like the rush of a mighty wind, and it filled all the house where they were sitting. And there appeared to them tongues as of fire, distributed and resting on each one of them. And they were all filled with the Holy Spirit and began to speak in other tongues, as the Spirit gave them utterance. (2:2-4)

It was a dramatic experience, one that galvanized them and changed their lives.

We can imagine how they felt.

A minister friend of mine told me about his experience with the Spirit. There was a Pentecostal church in his city, he said, achieving a wide reputation for worship services in which people were "slain in the Spirit." This phrase, in wide vogue among Pentecostalists, describes what happens when a person is touched by someone with special gifts for healing or changing the lives of others. When the person with the Spirit places a hand upon another, the second person is literally propelled backward as if struck a stunning blow. Usually in such services, assistants stand behind the people being touched to catch them when this occurs.

My friend had engaged in a public discussion of gifts of the Spirit and openly challenged a Pentecostal minister for having staged these "slain in the Spirit" episodes and thus behaving fraudulently. It was a heated debate, and my friend became angry and left, seething with hostility.

Later in his own church, he laid his hand gently upon a parishioner who came to him with a personal problem, and the person was suddenly knocked backward by a considerable force. Soon after, this occurred again with another parishioner. A third time, now in a mood of experimentation, he touched a woman who was having a problem, but with the precaution of slipping an arm around her waist, and *wham!*

"If I hadn't had my arm around her," he said, "she might have been badly hurt!"

My friend says that this experience, which has not been repeated in the years since, has greatly affected his attitude toward God and the Spirit. When he says the words "I believe in the Holy Spirit," he does so with understandable emphasis.

What is the background of this strange and powerful Spirit? Is it the divinity itself at work? Is it the spirit of Jesus, which he promised to send among the disciples?

We cannot pretend to have all the answers, as if we were reading the contents on a box of cereal. But the Bible gives us certain hints.

To begin with, the Spirit is mentioned in the opening verses of the Scriptures: "In the beginning God created the heavens and the earth. The earth was without form and void, and darkness was upon the face of the deep; and the Spirit of God was moving over the face of the waters" (Gen. 1:1-2).

In other words, the Spirit is identified as the creative power of God. I have always liked the way one old version of the Bible translated this: The Spirit "brooded upon the face of the deep." Brooding suggests something seminal and gestative, such as the reflective time through which an artist passes on the way to the act of creation.

In male/female terminology, it is possible to identify this creative side of God as what Carl Jung called the *anima*, the female principle that is the reproductive and nurturing aspect inside every male. If we would only learn to call the Holy Spirit "she" instead of "he" or "it," we might thus resolve the debate which modern studies of feminism have thrust upon us. It is very difficult—impossible, even—for a tradition that has always called God "the Father" suddenly to reverse itself and speak of God as "Mother." But it would not be too hard, I think, for most Christians to learn to regard the Spirit as Mother, for the work of the Spirit has been of the sort always identified with mothers.

Riane Eisler has shown in her remarkable book *The Chalice and the Blade* that all cultures, from prehistoric times onward, have had a strong and natural identification with a Great Mother figure; that our present culture, which she calls a dominator culture, with the emphasis on males and making war, is really only an aberration of the main line of cultural development. The sixteenth century, when Protestant Reformers redesigned their religion to omit homage to the virgin mother of Jesus as the mother of God, was one of the most male-dominated and warlike centuries in all history.

Now, says Eisler, we are at a moment of immense transformation in our cultural line, when new understandings of life and sexuality make it possible for us to restore the sense of partnership between male and female and once more pursue the life of peace and fullness of being known to our prehistoric and early historic ancestors.

It would be wonderful if the church, with a proper understanding of the Spirit as the mothering side of God, could contribute its considerable weight toward such an important thrust.

To return to our comments about the Spirit in the Bible, she is mentioned frequently throughout the Old Testament. It was God's Spirit that created and sustained the people of Israel. Psalm 51, the beautiful prayer of confession offered by David after his sin against Uriah, the husband of Bathsheba, beseeches:

> Create in me a clean heart, O God,
> and put a new and right spirit within me.
> Cast me not away from thy presence,
> and take not thy holy Spirit from me. (10-11)

The prophets often said that the Spirit of the Lord was essential to the well-being of the nation. One of the most important references is in the book of Joel, in which God is reported as saying,

And it shall come to pass afterward,
  that I will pour out my spirit on all flesh;
your sons and your daughters shall prophesy,
  your old men shall dream dreams,
  and your young men shall see visions.
Even upon the menservants and maidservants
  in those days, I will pour out my spirit. (2:28-29)

At Pentecost, the early Christians interpreted what had happened to them—the tongues of fire and speaking in other tongues—as a sign that God's Spirit had been poured out and that theirs was the age of the coming of the kingdom prophesied by Joel. As people will do, we have fastened upon those particular forms of manifestation, especially the tongue-speaking, and continue to look for the Spirit in this guise. But these probably were only temporary forms which the Spirit assumed. The important thing is the eruption of divine Spirit in the midst of their observance of Pentecost. The Spirit surely assumes whatever form she will, whenever she will, and we can expect other unusual signs of her presence in our midst today.

Many evidences appear, throughout the New Testament, of the early Christian understanding that God's Spirit was then among them. Mark says that when Jesus was baptized, "the heavens opened" and the Spirit descended on him "like a dove" (Mark 1:10). Luke reports that when Jesus addressed the elders in the synagogue in Nazareth, he announced, "The Spirit of the Lord is upon me, because he has anointed me to preach good news to the poor" (Luke 4:18). Paul writes frequently of being "in the Spirit" or "led by the Spirit." They were all convinced that the Spirit promised by Joel had come—that God was in their midst, creating a new heaven and a new earth.

Eduard Thurneysen, in *A Theology of Pastoral Care*, described the Spirit this way:

The Holy Spirit is indeed no other than God himself approaching us and grasping us; he is *our* God, the God acting *with* us and in us through his Word and choosing us to be his children. God is the Creator and Father *over* us; in his Son he is also *with* us, and in the Holy Spirit he is *in* us, in order to open our eyes and ears so that we learn to recognize, love, and fear him as our Father in his being with us in the Son.

All this is to say that Christians who have not learned to experience God as the Spirit are still in a preliminary state of faith. They do not yet know the *confidence* of faith, for they lack the sense that God is truly with them at all times. They are little acquainted with the true *community* of faith, for they have not felt the Spirit binding them together with others in the faith—both those they know and those who belong to the wider, ecumenical community of believers. And they are missing the *power* of faith, for they have not experienced God moving in and through them to correct human situations, heal the sick, or improve the world.

When I speak of the *confidence of faith,* I think of a friend who travels from country to country, witnessing to Christ wherever he goes. He stops among a group of Christians and carries their stories to the next group, and so on around the globe. He is like a wonderful honeybee, bearing pollen from flower to flower, making the world more beautiful. He has no money to speak of, but lives on the generosity of those he visits. Yet he never seems to lack for anything. When he is down to his last sou or pfennig or nickel, depending on where he is, something always provides for him.

"I live in the Spirit," he says. "God looks after me the way he looks after the sparrows. I have never gone to bed hungry!"

When I speak of *the community of faith,* I remember all the times I have gone to speak to some strange group of Christians miles from where I live. I always hate to go, for I enjoy being at home, and the trip to the airport is invariably a lonely experience. But when I get to the other end and meet the Christians who are awaiting my coming, it is another story. At once, we become friends and share intimately in the Spirit.

And as for *the power of faith*—my, one could hardly think of that without running mentally through the book of Acts and all those extraordinary events that occurred throughout the ministry of the apostles and early missionaries—healings, conversions, unusual appearances, and prison doors being opened! At one point, there was such enthusiasm among new converts to the faith that they carried their sick into the streets, so that the shadow of Peter might fall on them as he passed and heal them of their diseases and infirmities!

I am sure we don't make enough of healing in our churches today. We are so afraid of excesses, of being carried away by illusory methods or emphases.

But let me offer a little parenthesis of my own. For several years I had a hiatal hernia—a pesky condition in which part of the stomach occasionally wanders upward, becomes irritated, and causes much pain in the chest and back. It bothers me very infrequently, but when it does, it is as troublesome as a bus parked across the freeway.

On a recent Sunday morning I was having one of those bouts. When the moment came to enter the chancel for the morning prayer, I ascended the steps carefully, for sometimes the least movement can provoke an unwarranted attack of pain.

As I stood there with my back to the congregation, having my private prayers, I felt a special sense of presence at the altar.

"I am yours," I said, or something to that effect.

Suddenly I felt well—so well that I took a deep breath and simply relaxed. I could no longer feel the stressful condition in my chest. Instead, I merely felt at one with God. I turned and led the morning prayers with no further aggravation from the hernia.

I didn't say anything about it to my wife for a few days, lest it return. But it didn't. It was gone, just like that!

But my favorite recollection of the power of faith is a story I read many years ago in S. D. Gordon's *Quiet Talks on Prayer*. It was about D. L. Moody, a shoe clerk who became a great evangelist for Christ. At one time, Moody visited a small church in Great Britain. When he got up to speak during the morning service, he faced the coldest, most apathetic congregation he had ever seen, and he was glad when the experience was over. He dreaded going back again that evening, but unfortunately his presence had been advertised.

That evening service, though, was a totally different experience. As he preached, he noticed some warmth in the crowd. Then there was more warmth. Finally, there was so much warmth that a revival broke out and, though Moody was engaged to be somewhere else the next day, he promised to come back in a few days and continue to preach, so that the promise of that wonderful evening could be fulfilled.

When he returned, Moody learned what really had happened that unusual Sunday. An older woman in the congregation could no longer attend church, but spent her days in a wheelchair. When she first read about D. L. Moody and his great gifts as an evangelist, she had prayed that he would one day come to visit her little church. Then when a relative came home from church that Sunday morning and told her the preacher had been D. L. Moody from America, she had prayed all afternoon, asking God to send his Spirit upon the congregation and fill it with a desire for repentance and new life in Christ.

What happened that remarkable evening, said Moody, was not his doing. It was the work of that woman in her wheelchair, and of the powerful Spirit of God that had swept over the congregation, changing hearts and calling the entire church to new spiritual adventures.

Maybe it is this power that average Christians are so afraid of that we are reluctant to pray for the Spirit's presence. Everybody feels uneasy about taking hold of a firehose when a powerful blast of water is about to surge through it. But it is our failure to pray for the Spirit, and to live in the Spirit, that accounts for the terrible blight upon our churches today.

It isn't any wonder that people don't know what "I believe in the Holy Spirit" means, or that they can talk about it from only an intellectual or philosophical point of view.

The Spirit is *God among us,* and only the person who has *experienced* God among us truly comprehends what this means.

. . . the holy catholic church . . .

GOOD CHURCH,
BAD CHURCH

I am glad the creed does not say "I believe in the sinful local church," for then I should have to say, "I am sorry, but I cannot join you in this." While I believe in the "holy universal church" and have worked for it most of my life, I always have had a lover's quarrel with the church as it is, and I cannot say I would blame God very much, were it suddenly wiped from the face of the earth.

It is the sinful local church that has been responsible for a lot of bad press the church has received: the pride and pomp, the selfishness and insincerity, the prejudice and rigidity. All of us can tell tales of ignorance and hypocrisy in the church—ministers who were deceitful, deacons who were unbearable, men who were implacable, women who were silly and insufferable. Religion, says Anglican theologian H. A. Williams, is what many people do with their lunacy.

Many shameful episodes appear in the church's history: Crusades to recapture the Holy Land and free it from the "infidels"; Torquemada and the Spanish Inquisition; the persecution of the Reformers; the repressiveness of the Puritans; the religious arguments for the institution of slavery; the silence of European Christians when Hitler persecuted Jews; ecclesiastical capitulation to the power brokers in South Africa, and wherever else it is prudent to agree with the establishment; popular support of media evangelists who systematically exploit the poor and the ignorant; the long denial of equality to women within the structures of ecclesiastical preferment.

"Frankly," wrote Leslie Weatherhead in *The Christian Agnostic,* "I often wonder why so many people *do* go to church. Christianity must have a marvelous inherent power, or the churches would have killed it long ago."

"Jesus himself," an angry parishioner once said to me, "would not recognize the church as it is today."

I expect she was right.

Jesus founded a church that was small, simple, and passionate. It began when Simon Peter finally realized that Jesus was the Christ, the long-awaited Messiah sent from God, and said so in the presence of the other disciples.

"On this rock," said Jesus—presumably referring to Peter and the confession he had just offered—"I will build my church" (Matt. 16:18). And somehow the disciples understood this as a mandate, a divine expectancy that they give their lives to extend the community to as many as possible during their lifetime, and after that, that the work would be taken up by others and carried even farther, until it encompassed all the lands and peoples of the earth.

Almost from the beginning, though, there were troubles. Judas, one of the twelve, defected and betrayed the Master. Arguments arose among the others about which was greatest. Within a few years of Jesus' death, a great rift occurred over whether people had to become Jews in order to be Christians. Paul wrote to the church at Corinth to chide the members for jealousy, competition, and carnality. John wrote of the church at Sardis that it was dead (Rev. 3:1) and of the church at Laodicea that it was so lukewarm in its faith that God would spew it out of his mouth! (Rev. 3:16).

As many have surely said in every age, the church would be wonderful if it weren't for the people in it. It is the people—the congregated sinners—who besmirch the ideal of a "holy universal church" and turn it into the "sinful local church."

"Each one of you," Paul accused the Corinthians, "says, 'I belong to Paul,' or 'I belong to Apollos,' or 'I belong to Cephas,' or

'I belong to Christ.' Is Christ divided? Was Paul crucified for you? Or were you baptized in the name of Paul?" (1:12-13). He was confronting the human urge to divide, to segregate, to create factions and denominations.

What guilt the denominational leaders—and the most ardent followers of denominations—will face when they stand before the throne and hear the eternal Judge say, "What place does factionalism have in my kingdom?"

I have always been a great admirer of Simone Weil, the brilliant Alsatian writer and philosopher who long refused to become a member of the church, even though she believed in and loved the church, because she said it would separate her from her many friends, some of whom belonged to other churches and some to none at all.

She would have understood the question of the Japanese customs official who was trying to discover the religious preference of an American traveler who said he was a Christian. "What *damnation?*" the official asked. "What *damnation?*"

A similar urge among those who comprise the church seems to identify the success of the kingdom of God with buildings—the stone-and-mortar campuses of convents and seminaries and local congregations.

The early church had no such campuses, of course; it met in synagogues and homes and groves and caves—wherever a little band of believers could be safely accommodated. And some believe it was then truer to its purpose, and to awaiting the arrival of the divine rulership, than it has been since the time of Constantine and the wave of church building that followed his edict that established Christianity as a legal religion in the Holy Roman Empire.

A popular story about reformer Martin Luther claims that his sense of revulsion at kneeling while climbing the steps of St. Peter's Basilica—the costly new world headquarters of the Roman church being erected in Rome—led the crusty young Augustinian monk from Germany to go home and start the Protestant Reformation. Some would argue that his revulsion proceeded from a theological difference with Rome; others think it had to do with the worldliness and grandeur of the pope's life in Italy.

"One thing is sure," said a friend whose congregation holds its weekly meetings in a schoolhouse. "We don't have any members who confuse buildings with Christianity. People don't bother with us unless they are willing to carry in baby beds on Sunday and worship God in a room with a chalkboard."

Kagawa said that religions should concentrate on people, not on buildings. Buildings, he remarked, are like the shells of mollusks, which grow around the organism and are then abandoned. The life is in the organism, not in the shell. To devote too much time and energy to maintain the shell is foolish; worse, it is obscene.

"Well would it be," said that great Japanese Christian, "if the world's churches and temples were razed to the ground. Then possibly we would understand genuine religion."

What would he have written if he could have heard what I once heard when someone innocently suggested that a certain church building cost too much to repair and perhaps should be abandoned for a newer, less expensive building. A trustee declared: "I love this church [building], and I would give my soul and the souls of everybody else in this room for the sake of this church!"

Add to the problem of factionalism and our devotion to buildings the unbearable dullness of a lot of religion. Suppose that you, a stranger, enter an "average" worship service somewhere in the United States. The congregation is singing a hymn written by some third-rate poet more than two hundred years ago, in the age of poetic diction. It may contain some indecipherable line such as "here I raise mine Ebenezer" or "where Eden's bowers bloom," which none but the initiated can understand. The prayers are hackneyed and uninspired. The sermon is poorly composed and monotonously delivered, and as someone once put it, without enough gospel to save a titmouse. You may think you have entered a time-warp or are experiencing a cranial disconnection, and you wonder what obsession or attachment can bring people back week after week for such dull and unendurable punishment.

And the people themselves! How uncompromising and unkind and unconverted they can be! If we wonder how Judas could have betrayed Jesus after being with him for three years or more, we have only to look at these people. Some have been members of the church for thirty, forty, fifty years, and still seem no mellower, no more loving and forgiving, no more Christlike than when they entered years ago. If anything, they have used their understanding of the Christian faith to bend and manipulate others to their wills.

I once met a pastor whose wife had had a stroke and had become a human vegetable.

"How difficult for you," I exclaimed when I heard it. "But surely the church members have been a great support to you."

They were at first, the pastor told me, and brought around casseroles and jars of soup. But after a few months they began to resent their pastor spending the time with an invalid that they thought he should be spending at his work. They made derogatory remarks within his hearing and often suggested that it was time he left and found another church to pastor.

All this has to do with what one writer has called the spotted reality of the church's existence—the impure congregation, the less than perfect performance record, the disparity between what we say we believe and how we actually behave.

Yet, despite everything, Jesus said that nothing could stop the church, not even the "powers of death" (Matt. 16:18).

Of course there is division in the church. It is composed of human beings, and human beings are notoriously fractious.

But the church will prevail!

Of course we have confused our buildings and altar furniture with the kingdom of God. We have our "edifice" complexes just like everybody else, and we forget that the Spirit does not dwell in earthly houses.

But the church will prevail!

Of course our worship services are often dull and unimposing.

Christians are not necessarily more imaginative than reporters and lawyers and members of civic clubs.

But the church will prevail!

Of course the people who comprise our congregations are sometimes mean and heartless and insensitive to the needs of others. Jesus had trouble keeping his own disciples in line, and there were only a dozen of them.

But the church will prevail!

Why will it prevail? Not because it is perfect. Not because its liturgies are so compelling that no one can resist them. Not because its members are so loving and true that everyone wants to join and be like them. But because it is based on the confession that Jesus is the Christ, and because he said it will prevail!

It's as simple as that.

Jesus is our Lord, and as long as anybody recognizes that fact, the church will continue to exist.

Where else in our world, I ask you, is the gospel kept alive? Where else do people acknowledge that God is the Creator of all things and that the Creator has lovingly sought all the wayward children, to bring them home to the warmth and joy of the family where they belong? We may have the treasure in earthen vessels, as Paul put it—in crackable pottery—but where else does it appear at all?

Only in the church and its extensions throughout the world can people hear about God's forgiveness for their sins and be drawn into the service of the Kingdom, which will one day supersede the kingdoms of this world. The church has changed and is changing the world. There is much to be done, inside the church as well as outside it. But no other body, no other organization, has been given the commission Christ gave the church, to go into all the world, teaching and preaching and baptizing into one family the peoples of all nations.

We admit we have failed. There isn't any pastor or congregation or individual Christian in the world who ought not to bow down in shame and say, "Lord, I'm sorry, I was not worthy of this great trust." But the church has not died, and the church *won't* die. Not the real church. Oh, individual churches will die. People will fail to preach the gospel, and they will grow old and tired and pass from the scene, and their church buildings will fall into disrepair and be turned into warehouses or torn down to make room for new buildings of various kinds. But the church of Jesus Christ will not die.

Denominations will come and go. They will flourish for a while and look prosperous in the eyes of their adherents, and then they will care more about their programs and appearances than they care about God and people, and they will fade and die. But the church of Jesus Christ will not die. It will continue to live, if only in the hearts of poor, elderly folk and in the hearts of the homeless and in the hearts of illiterate natives in developing nations. Not even the "powers of death" will prevail against it, for Christ himself has promised.

Meanwhile, it is important that we continue to believe in the church—in the holy universal church, if not in the sinful local church. And perhaps believing in the holy universal church will continue to bring us back again and again to the sinful local church, to pray for it and uphold it and struggle with it to convert it into the holy universal church. In this life, nothing is really holy or universal. Not in its entirety. It only participates, with varying success, in the holy and universal. But in that sense, it has a claim upon us and draws us again and again, just as we are drawn to marriage, despite the fact that there are no perfect marriages; just as we are drawn to the theater, despite the fact that there are no perfect plays.

In the end, we need to ask where we would be if there were no church; if the disciples of Jesus had failed, and no gospel had reached the people of the second century; if God had become disgusted because of the Inquisition or the excesses of Puritanism and had wiped out the church; if some imperfect witness, arising from some imperfect congregation in some imperfect surroundings, had not reached us with the message of God's love and redemption for our wounded, broken lives. We cannot turn away from the church because of its failures. To do so would be to miss everything it has meant to us, and is still capable of meaning, if we will only yield ourselves to the Christ who is its Lord.

George Docherty, who for many years was pastor of New York Avenue Presbyterian Church in Washington, D. C., tells of a pastoral call he made when he was a minister in Aberdeen, Scotland. A woman who belonged to his church asked him to come to dinner and talk with her husband, who was not a churchgoer. They lived, said George, in a little jerry-built house in the suburbs. But in the back was a fabulous garden the husband had tended, with grass "like a billiard table" and roses and fruit trees, and even a bird singing in one of the trees.

The dinner was at 6:00, and at 10:00, George got around to the reason for his call.

"Sandy," he said to the husband, "why don't you come to church?"

"Oh, I dinna need to come," said Sandy. "My garden is all the church I need."

Sometime later, the woman became ill and died. When George went to call on her husband, he saw that the garden, once so beautiful, had grown up in weeds and thorns.

"Sandy," said George, "what good is your garden now?" And he began to tell him about another garden, where Jesus prayed and found God's will for his life; and another, where Jesus was buried and rose from the grave.

Where would we be without the church?

FRIENDS
IN HIGH PLACES

A missionary doctor to Zaire had visited a jungle outpost, and his car broke down in the darkness as he was driving home. Knowing that many patients would be waiting for him the next morning and that no one was likely to come along the single-track road, he decided to walk through the jungle. As he walked, he heard voices ahead. Fearful that the voices might be those of headhunters, he approached cautiously. When he was close enough to see the natives sitting around a campfire, he realized they were singing a familiar tune. He knew enough Tscilupa, the local language, to recognize some of the words. They were singing "What a Friend We Have in Jesus"! The doctor joined them and sang with them, and one of the men later accompanied him to be sure he arrived home safely.

A military chaplain serving in the South Pacific during World War Two was sent to visit a tribe of people who had been relocated on another island because our government was testing the atomic bomb near the island where they had lived. When the chaplain and his assistant arrived in a PT boat, they were greeted by the tribe, but did not understand the language. Communication seemed all but impossible. Then one chaplain began to sing a hymn. To their amazement, the natives joined in, singing in their own language. For almost a week, they communicated principally through the singing of hymns. When the two Americans got in their boat to leave, the smiling natives stood on the beach, singing their own rendition of "God Be With You Till We Meet Again."

Both these examples—one in Africa, the other in the South Pacific—are illustrations of what the Apostles' Creed means when it speaks of believing in "the communion of saints." The phrase embodies a sense of the network of believers around the world, a community that reaches beyond political and sociological boundaries to embrace all followers of the Lord Jesus Christ.

The theme is well expressed in John Oxenham's majestic hymn, "In Christ There Is No East or West":

> In Christ there is no east or west,
>   in him no south or north;
> but one great fellowship of love
>   throughout the whole wide earth.
>
> In Christ shall true hearts everywhere
>   their high communion find;
> his service is the golden cord
>   close binding humankind.
>
> In Christ now meet both east and west,
>   in him meet south and north;
> all Christly souls are one in him
>   throughout the whole wide earth.

The New Testament refers to such an ideological community in many ways. In the Fourth Gospel, Jesus speaks of abiding in him and loving one another more than our own lives (ch. 15). The book of Hebrews says that we are surrounded by a "cloud of witnesses"—all the faithful of the ages—and should therefore "run with perseverance the race that is set before us" (12:1c). The Johannine epistles stress the importance of love within the family of believers. Paul consistently sent greetings to friends in Christ in all the churches he visited, and declared in his letter to the Galatians that because we are all in Christ, there is now neither Jew nor Greek, slave nor free, male nor female, but we are caught up in a universal fellowship that recognizes none of the former boundaries! (3:28).

Ultimately, such an understanding derives from the idea of the oneness of God and of the loving equality with which God regards all of us. Louis Evely, the Belgian Catholic, puts it this way: "Why is our religion a religion of community? Because God is community." Indeed, the early church understood its koinonia, or fellowship, to spring from its rootedness in God. If God is one, then God's people also are one.

Thomas Merton's *Life and Holiness* clearly indicates that he understood the community of saints in this way. The church is more than the sum of its apparent constituents, he said; it is a "mystical body." If I wish to know God's will for my life, I can discern it as much from the mystical body as from anything. I merely ask, "What will be good for the community of God's people?" God and the community are so inseparable that to know what the community needs is to know what God wants.

This is why Bede Griffiths, the British writer, found living in a monastery so important. The monastery, he said, is a model for life in the church, in the entire community of God. There, by submitting ourselves to others and drawing upon their love and insights, we discover our true identities and find our greatest understanding of God.

But if God is really community and we all dwell in some mystical way in God, then another dimension of our relationship must be explored, and that is the eternal, or spiritual, dimension. Since God is not limited to temporal relationships—relationships that exist within a single period of time—then we must, through God, be related to all the saints who ever lived or ever will live. Jesus said to the Sadducees that God "is not God of the dead, but of the living" (Matt. 22:32)—that is, God is somehow *presently* God of all those who have lived, including Abraham, Isaac, and Jacob, whom Jesus specifically mentioned. In some mystical way, then, we are related to all these figures, as well as to the Christian natives of Zaire or the South Sea islands. The image of a "cloud of witnesses" suggests as much, as does the book of Revelation when it pictures all the saints gathered around the high throne of God.

What does this really mean?

Perhaps it has something to do with what a woman told me about a dream she had:

I was going through a very anxious period. My husband had left me, and my only child was living abroad. I had a persistent illness and was worried about having enough money to see me through if I really fell ill and couldn't work. On top of everything, I was having trouble sleeping. Then one night I had this very gripping dream. It was so real that it didn't go away when I awoke. I dreamed that I was walking in a meadow with a woman I had never met before. She was very beautiful, and her voice was calm and deep, like the voice of a wonderful actress. Somehow, I knew that the meadow was heaven, or at least a heavenly place. And the woman said to me as we walked along, "You have many friends here; you do not need to be afraid."

I felt strangely calm and peaceful when I awoke, and the calm and peace have never left me. If I begin to become anxious, I pause and think about the dream and the woman who said I didn't need to be afraid. I *do* have many friends there. I know it, and it comforts me.

Another woman, a medical doctor, told me a similar thing about her father, who had died, but had appeared to her in a dream more than once during a time of need.

"He told me," she said, "that I shouldn't ever worry; he would be there. And I don't worry. I know he's there."

What these experiences suggest, you see, is very much in line with what the scriptures themselves say—that we are not alone, but live in a kind of eternal community, where we are cared for by others who also draw their strength from God.

Our only difficulty is in learning to trust the community and to rely on it in faith. This problem is easily understood. From childhood, we have learned *not* to trust others. Our parents taught us not to get into cars with strangers or accept food from people we didn't know. Experiences with classmates taught us that we could not share secrets and expect them to be kept, especially if they were of a personal nature. We learned not to leave possessions of value where others had access to them. We developed the habit of not confiding to others our deepest feelings, lest they use that knowledge to betray or control us. In short, we learned to be cynics, believing that a healthy distrust is the surest way to get along in the world.

It doesn't matter where you turn, the tone of the response is the same.

"I don't open my door to anyone," says the housewife.

"It's a dog-eat-dog world," says the businessman.

"I don't trust my own mother," says the student.

"I keep my back to the wall and don't tell anything I don't want told," says the typical employee.

How do we learn, in such a world, to reverse the trend and begin to trust again?

One thing is sure—we must work at it!

During the sixties and seventies, a number of U. S. business firms, suspecting that a more trustful atmosphere would make their employees more productive, undertook programs to inspire trust and reliance, especially at the executive and junior executive levels. A friend who was vice-president of an insurance company described some of their meetings.

We had a number of retreats in a nearby state park. The company brought in sensitivity trainers who worked with us for two days at a time. For example, they had us stand around in a circle, with one of us in the middle. The person in the middle had to fall backward and depend on the group to catch him. At first, you were reluctant to let go and do it. But after you'd done it a time or two and realized the others wouldn't let you fall, it got to be fun, and you could do it with a sense of pleasure.

We also did what they called "blind walks." That was when some of us were blindfolded and then led out through the park by others. It was kind of scary at first, because you figured you would stumble over a tree root or a curb or something. But then, when you learned that your partner was watching out for you, you learned to relax and enjoy it as an adventure.

I asked if the effects of such training were very ephemeral, or if they lasted a long time.

"Oh, definitely a long time," said my friend. "Sometimes I still think about those exercises, and they remind me that there is a basic goodwill in most people which we don't tap often enough. It helps me to be more trusting of those I'm working with, and when I am, they come through more positively for me."

Suppose that one could learn to trust the communion of saints that way—just lean back and let it take over. Wouldn't that help us relax, make life easier for us? Wouldn't it lower our stress level, so our own adrenaline could take over and do a better job in the situations we face?

Imagine, if you will, that you are pretty well at the end of your rope. For the past several weeks, circumstances have conspired to make your life hard. Tensions have your stomach knotted up, and you can't think clearly. You aren't sleeping well and don't know how much longer you can go on.

Then you remember the communion of saints—all the people of faith who have walked this way before you, and the others who are walking it now in other parts of the world—and you know that there is a residual power for good in them. God hears their prayers and ministers to the world through them.

You decide to trust them with your problems. It is as if you mentally gathered up your problems and handed them over to specific saints you have thought about—perhaps one of the characters of the Bible or a member of your family who is in heaven, or maybe a good friend who has promised to pray for you and help carry your burdens.

The instant you make the resolution and act on it, you begin to feel better. Your load is lightened. Your mind eases and begins to clear. "By golly," you think, "I can make it now. Someone is helping me with this thing!"

Try it. You will see that it works.

The more you do it, the more practiced you become, the more natural it feels.

It will become *living* theology to you, as opposed to mere academic theology. That is, you will experience God as community in your life, and know that your strength as a Christian comes from God and the others who make up the family of Christ. It doesn't come from inside yourself; it comes from them.

I could not count the number of times I have heard or read of someone in prison or in the hospital or in dire straits of another kind who said, "I never would have made it, were it not for thinking about so-and-so and knowing that he or she was thinking about me and praying for me. I felt the strength flow into me, and it saved my life."

An Anglican friend said, "You know, we sometimes have prayers for the dead in our liturgy, when we pray for those who have gone on to be with God. But I always think, when we are praying for them, that they are praying for us as well, and it strengthens me."

This is what the business of having patron saints is about in the Catholic church. Particular saints are supposed to watch over one on a journey, during childbirth, in an illness, in military service, or in other times of trouble or danger. Normally, in this teaching, the saint is one who was especially meritorious, and is therefore considered to have unusual power with God.

But the phrase "communion of saints" is much broader and more inclusive. Derived from the Greek word *koinonia*, which means "household" or "fellowship," it implies the entire collective life of the saints—all those living and dead who are in God. Even the *smallest* saint is important in God's sight and can be an important friend in time of need.

I used to wonder why the creed does not say anything about love. Love is so important in the Christian's life. Paul described it in his letter to the Corinthians as the crowning glory of our existence, the single quality that outranks and outlasts all others. Yet the creed is mysteriously silent about it.

Then one day I was praying and thinking about the saints in heaven—especially my mother—who were praying for me, and I realized, "Love is there! It is in the community of saints! That's what the communion of saints is all about! It's why Jesus, at the last supper, talked about abiding in him and loving one another at the same time. They belong together—being in him and loving." That's the real meaning of the communion of saints, and most of the time we forget it and neglect to draw our strength from it.

Wyatt Cooper, in his book *Families*, tells about the time he took his young son to a family reunion in Mississippi. After "dinner on the ground," one of those huge southern feasts, he led the boy to the old family cemetery, where they pulled back the ivy and read the inscriptions on the tombstones. He wanted his son to be conscious of his family in a world where people live increasingly alone and without families. He wanted him to draw strength from them and know that he was a part of something bigger than himself.

That's what the communion of saints is about. It means we are part of something bigger than ourselves and that we can draw strength from it. It means that we are all parts of God, that we are never alone.

THE POSITIVE POWER
OF FORGIVENESS

Some people have an obvious need for forgiveness: the distraught mother who couldn't stand her child's crying and finally burned the child's hand in an open flame; the alcoholic whose dependency ruined the lives of his children and eventually led to the breakup of the family; the power-crazed lieutenant who, during the war in Vietnam, ordered the unnecessary destruction of an entire village; the scam artist who bilked hundreds of elderly people out of their savings; the serial killer who murdered a dozen women in Los Angeles.

I was only twelve when my sister was killed by an old farm truck that ran off the road after its brakes failed on a downhill curve. But I remember clearly the day the driver, who had spent the night in jail, stood at our front door, hat in hand, to ask my father's forgiveness for his negligence. My father told him he did not bear any malice, and it seemed to lift a great weight from the man's conscience.

But the point Jesus makes again and again in the Gospels is that forgiveness is not something needed only by people who have committed very obvious sins, but is something needed by *everybody* all the time. It is not the special preserve of those who have dramatically erred—crooks and prostitutes and murderers—but the daily requirement of average people, people like ourselves, who may not have any strong sense of wrongdoing.

You will remember the story of the paraplegic who was carried to Jesus and let down through the roof because of the great crowd of people. The first thing Jesus did, after this surprising entry, was to *forgive* the man. Now, if you reflect on it, that is rather amazing. What great sin could that poor fellow have committed, being bedfast? There are not many Commandments he could have broken, for some of those require a fair amount of mobility. But Jesus forgave him, which suggests that there are always sins of the heart that do not demand any social interaction for fulfillment.

And we know Jesus' famous parable about the Pharisee and the publican, two very different men who went to the temple to pray. The Pharisee, who worked hard at living righteously every day—Robert Burns might have called him one of the "unco guid," or uncommonly good persons—stood before the holy altar and thanked God that his life was unsullied, which was more than he could say for the tax collector he saw kneeling nearby. The tax collector, a virtual outcast in the Jewish community, bewailed his degraded status and begged God to have mercy on his soul.

Jesus gave a twist to the story that ought to go straight to the heart of every one of us.

That poor man, he said—the tax collector—went home with God's approval, while the Pharisee didn't, because the Pharisee was blind to his own need to be forgiven. The Pharisee was such a good man, in his own eyes and the eyes of the community, that it simply didn't enter his mind to ask for God's forgiveness.

That should make us think—especially those of us who haven't recently felt any guilt and haven't bothered to beseech God for our own forgiveness. Maybe we even said the Lord's Prayer—"forgive our sins as we forgive those who sin against us"—without a ripple of consciousness, thinking, "Of course I don't really have any sins right now."

What it's all about, you see, is our being *dynamically rejoined to God and the community of holiness through God's active forgiveness at every moment of our consciousness*. It isn't that God is angry and is sulking because we are sinners. It is simply that what Kierkegaard called "an infinite qualitative distance" lies between us and God and that we should bear this in mind at all times and, whenever we think of it, seek God's forgiveness for this distance and be spiritually rejoined to the Holy Spirit.

Perhaps it is a little like being the guests of a very wealthy, aristocratic person of great fame at that person's summer estate. It is unlikely that any of us would forget our station, so to speak, or cease to be filled with wonder and gratitude to our host for the privilege of being there. Whenever we met, on the terrace or at dinner or in the library, we would feel appropriately deferential, and our speech would convey our sense of humility. We would not dream, in such a situation, of being cavalier or unnoticing; our whole intention would be to appear as attentive and grateful as possible, and thereby maintain as much intimacy with our benefactor as could be expected of persons of our rank and background.

That is an insufficient illustration, but it may point in the right direction. God has indeed shown his love to us. But we ought not, on this account, to forget our proper deference to God's holiness. We should maintain a great sensitivity to God's presence and to our incalculable debt, and this should lead us to a continuing desire for forgiveness and acceptance.

But it is not only of God that we should desire forgiveness, said Jesus; it is of other human beings as well. Just as we are not whole when there is distance between us and God, we are not whole when there is distance between us and other persons. Therefore, said Jesus, "if you are offering your gift at the altar, and there remember that your brother has something against you, leave your gift there before the altar and go; first be reconciled to your brother, and then come and offer your gift" (Matt. 5:23-24).

If someone needs our forgiveness, by the same token, we should not make it difficult for that person to receive it. "For if you forgive men their trespasses," said Jesus, "your heavenly Father also will forgive you; but if you do not forgive men their trespasses, neither will your Father forgive your trespasses" (Matt. 6:14-15).

In fact, said Jesus on another occasion, the kingdom of heaven itself is like a king who found that one of his servants owed him a staggering debt. When the man could not pay it, the king forgave him. But when the servant was unable to extract payment of a much smaller debt another man owed him, he had the man thrown into prison. The king then called the servant in and had *him* imprisoned because he was not forgiving, as the king had been (Matt. 18:23-35).

It is interesting that Jesus would say that this is like the kingdom of heaven—a society of mutual forgiveness, of renewed fellowship and intimacy, based on God's forgiving us and our forgiving one another.

As I suggested before, it all has to do with a kind of psychic *wholeness,* with our being part of the entire community of God in such a gentle and loving way that no enmity exists among us. This wholeness is so important that we should actively seek it at all times—first by praying regularly and sincerely for our own forgiveness, and then by giving it freely among other human beings. God's wrath erupts against those who withhold their forgiveness, but God's community is also denied to those who do not seek it for themselves.

The question is, Who can afford to live without this forgiveness daily?

Let me share my personal experience. As I was writing this chapter, I realized for the first time the importance of daily—even hourly—forgiveness. Forgiveness is more than pardon for particular sins; it is an affirmation of God's holiness and God's acceptance of me as a finite human being who desires fellowship with God. When the realization occurred, I immediately began to pray for forgiveness.

Here I was, a clergyman who spends most of his hours working on sermons and prayers, counseling people, dealing with the poor, and generally trying to conduct ministry; and I confess I had been rather self-content. I didn't puff myself up; it was simply that I work at rather respectable undertakings all day, and most evenings as well, and had never especially regarded myself as a sinner. But when I saw the point of Jesus' teaching about forgiveness—that it is not the bad person who needs it so much as the basically good person who assumes that he or she doesn't—I suddenly knew that my attitude had been entirely too self-complacent and that I did indeed need to ask God's forgiveness.

I was not prepared for the sudden sense of energizing—as if, with this radical turnabout in my own attitude, I was immediately brought into intimacy with God again. I experienced a renewal I had not counted on. Like an electric plug that had been disconnected, when I prayed for forgiveness, it was as if I had been plugged in again, and the current of God's Spirit once more flowed through my life.

I now realize that I need this every day—not just occasionally or in special seasons. This must be why Jesus placed "Forgive us our sins" immediately after "Give us today our daily bread" in the Lord's Prayer. There is a dailiness about the act of forgiveness, just as about receiving physical nourishment.

I also saw why, in the Apostles' Creed, belief in "the forgiveness of sins" follows hard on the heels of "the communion of saints." It is the forgiveness of sins that reunites us to the koinonia, the community of believers and God. The renewed power and grace I experienced came from being reattached to the whole and feeling the power and grace of the whole coursing through my spiritual self.

One of the finest descriptions of the working of forgiveness is contained in *Sangster of Westminster* by H. C. Pawson—a sermon by W. E. Sangster, the great pastor of Westminster Central Hall in London. Sangster asked the people in the congregation to imagine that all the "undesirable things" in their minds were loaded on a "sludge vessel" and dropped at sea.

Sludge vessels are a most important part of the sanitary system of London. When millions of people congregate together in one city, it takes little imagination to realise that the maintenance of their health is a vast problem. . . .

Not all sewage is waste. . . . But, when every use has been made of the city's refuse, there remains an irreducible and dangerous sediment called sludge. . . .

London has four sludge vessels. They are tankers really, with a cargo-carrying capacity of 1,500 tons. On every weekday tide, two of the sludge vessels set out laden with this unwanted and perilous matter and travel down the Thames to Black Deep, a depression on the bed of the ocean, fifteen miles off Foulness. When the vessel reaches Black Deep, the valves are opened and the complete cargo runs out in about twenty minutes. Down it goes, down into the salt aseptic sea. A dark stain spreads over the wake of the ship, but so wide is the ocean, and so deep the declivity, and so briny the sea that, within one hour, samples of water taken either from the surface of the sea, or the bed of the estuary, prove to be completely innocuous. The sludge has gone, devitalised of all evil power, and never to be seen again. It has sunk from all human ken in the cavernous hollow of Black Deep, and has lost its evil nature on the way.

The comparison is obvious: God's love is the Black Deep where our sins are dropped and buried for all eternity. What else could we do with our evil, our failure, our rebellion, our insincerity, our unfaith? Only one thing will get rid of it. God must bear it away. God, who is holiness. God, who is righteousness. God must bear away our sins and sink them in the depths of love, where they will be purified and made sweet again.

Do you see the power of forgiveness? It is the power to be renewed, to feel cleansed, to know we are restored to God's favor and to wholeness in the community God is building. It isn't a negative power at all, but a positive power. In fact, it is the most positive power in the world. Nothing else can rebuild a life the way it can. Nothing else can so change the life of an individual or a nation. Forgiveness is a dynamo, waiting to regenerate our lives.

But we must see this. We must see it and realize that the garbage need not pile up in our lives. Our psyches don't need to be full of refuse. God's sludge vessels are waiting to take away the irreducible filth and decay of our existence. All we need to do is realize this and say, "Here, Lord, I yield myself to you. Take away my sin through the mystery of your love, and receive me into oneness with you and your divine community."

And lo and behold, it is done.

In the twinkling of an eye.

THE SEED OF SOMETHING WONDERFUL

I was talking with a friend whose father-in-law had died a few months before.

"How is your wife feeling about her father's death?" I asked.

"It's funny you should ask," he said. "Last night in the middle of dinner, she began to cry. We had had a beautiful day. In fact, we had spent most of the day planting flowers. Then suddenly without any warning, she just began to cry. I said, 'What's the matter, honey?' She said, 'I was thinking about Daddy. I'm afraid he's cold out there in the ground.'"

It sounded very familiar. The day after my wife's mother was buried, my wife said, "I woke up worrying about Mama. I thought, 'What's going to happen when it rains? Mama will get wet down there in the grave.'"

Letting go of the earthly body is not easy, is it? We have deep attachments to it. We cannot imagine what it will be like to transcend the body, to leave it behind.

Maybe this is why some people do patently foolish things on the way to death. Before she died, a terminally ill woman had her hair set by a professional hairdresser every day for three months so that she would look her best in death. One man who had never paid more than $200 for a suit, knowing he had only a few months to live, spent $5,000 to fly a tailor from New York and have an Italian suit made for his corpse. Another woman signed a contract with her plastic surgeon and her undertaker, providing that when she died the surgeon was to assist the undertaker in making whatever skin tucks were necessary to make her look younger in her casket.

It is a paradox, wrote world-religions scholar Mircea Eliade in *No Souvenirs:*

The Greeks, who . . . loved life, existence in the flesh, the perfect form, had, as an ideal of survival, the survival of the pure intellect (mind, *nous*). Christians, who are apparently ascetics and scorn the body, insist on the necessity of the resurrection of the body, and cannot conceive of paradisiac blessedness without the union of the soul and the body.

The paradox lies deep within our faith. Our bodies, we are taught, can easily mislead us in life. They can divert our attention from matters of love and faithfulness that work for our eternal salvation. At the same time, we believe that we somehow shall survive death, that we shall retain a form of consciousness on the other side of life, and we cannot imagine this without the bodies in which we have always resided. Our bodies are part of who we are. They help to form our personalities. They affect our feelings from day to day. Flesh and soul have become so entwined over the years that we fear their extrication. We cannot imagine life without some form of the body.

And neither could Christians in the earliest years of the church. "How are the dead raised?" they asked when Paul preached about resurrection. "With what kind of body do they come?" (I Cor. 15:35).

Those who asked these questions were Greeks, people who had been raised in the best traditions of hellenistic thought. That philosophy taught, as Eliade implied, a strict dualism between the mind and body. The mind was like an ethereal bird imprisoned in the body. When the body died, the bird was free to fly away. Only, to them, this was not a joyous occasion. Because they were so wed to the life of aesthetics and the life of the flesh, they could not imagine an existence for the mind that would be pleasurable without the body. They pictured the mind as living on in a kind of gloomy underworld, devoid of interest and happiness.

The idea of resurrection must have struck them with great promise, but they could not begin to comprehend it.

How? they asked.

If there is actually a resurrection, what kind of body does it produce?

"Aphrown!" says Paul.

"Fool!"

"Simpleton!"

"What you sow does not come to life unless it dies. And what you sow is not the body which is to be, but a bare kernel, perhaps of wheat or of some other grain" (I Cor. 15:36*b*-37).

There's the trick, isn't it? What we shall be when we die is somehow contained in who we are while we live, but it is more than that. Just as the apple tree comes from the apple seed and the peach tree from the peach seed—from the very seed that dies, not from some seed-in-general—so we shall come from the body-minds we are now; but as the apple tree is far more than the seed from which it grew, and the peach tree more than the seed from which it sprang, so we shall be far more than anyone could tell by looking at us now.

It is intriguing to think what we shall be and that it is somehow related to who and what we presently are. Perhaps this is why the ethical teachings of our religion are so important: Our adherence to them defines us not only in the lives we now live but in our lives to come. If we have learned to live in the Spirit, as Paul says, so that our existence is characterized by "love, joy, peace, patience, kindness, goodness, faithfulness, gentleness, self-control," and not by "fornication, impurity, licentiousness, idolatry, sorcery, enmity, strife, jealousy, anger, selfishness, dissension, party spirit, envy, drunkenness, carousing, and the like," then we are bound to produce beautiful lives in eternity (Gal. 5:22-23, 19*b*-21*a*).

I knew a man who was afraid to die because, as he himself said, he had lived as Ebenezer Scrooge did before his conversion: "I know I shall go hobbled and manacled into the life to come, like some shameful criminal who has plundered the earth of its gifts and returned nothing." Fortunately he, like Scrooge, saw the error of his ways and began to live much differently before he died. His spirit became so sweet and generous that I am sure God was generous also and gave him a good "body" after death. He proved that the seed was really there.

I said that God gave the man a body. That is not my idea, you know; it is what Paul said in his first letter to the Corinthians. We sow the seed, he wrote, and then "God gives it the sort of body that he has chosen for it, and for each kind of seed its own kind of body" (15:38 NJB). Receiving a heavenly body is not automatic. It is not something everybody has a right to. *God gives it.*

This is where Christian teaching differs from other teachings about immortality. Immortality is a Greek concept; it means that life goes on automatically, at least in some form, forever. But the Christian teaching is about resurrection. Resurrection means that someone must do the raising. And that someone is God. God raises the dead in Christ. God performs an overt act by making the dead seed blossom into a heavenly plant.

Without God's loving grace, it would not happen. Thus the emphasis on eternal life is kept where it ought to be, centered on God and God's power. We have no automatic right to live forever. But God wills that those who have been saved through his Son Jesus have an eternal form beyond this life.

And what a form it will be!

Listen to Paul. He has been talking about the seed and the plant that springs from it—and that the plant is much more remarkable than the seed. Now he says:

It is the same too with the resurrection of the dead: what is sown is perishable, but what is raised is imperishable; what is sown is contemptible but what is raised is glorious; what is sown is weak, but what is raised is powerful; what is sown is a natural body, and what is raised is a spiritual body. (I Cor. 15:42-44 NJB)

Notice the adjectives! The body that dies is *perishable, contemptible, weak.* We know that, don't we? Especially if we are among the aging population. The older we become, the more perishable, contemptible, and weak we think ourselves. The parts of the body, like the parts of an old machine, begin to wear out and cause dysfunction of the whole. They embarrass us by calling a disproportionate amount of attention to themselves.

My wife bought a birthday card for a friend. "Growing old," it declared, "is pigeon poop!"

We understand that.

And it isn't always the old who feel that their bodies are perishable, contemptible, and weak. Sometimes the young feel the same, especially if they are not robust or suffer from some debilitating disease.

But the physical body is only the seed; the body that is raised up—the spiritual body—is another story!

It is *imperishable, glorious,* and *powerful.* Think of that, if you have ever despised the body you now have; your spiritual body will be imperishable, glorious, and powerful!

It will be imperishable—it will never die. No accident or illness can touch it. It will never be susceptible to termination. It will go on forever.

It will be glorious, like the *Hallelujah Chorus* in the flesh, embodied in a person. Like the sun breaking over the Rocky Mountains in the early morning or settling its colorful petticoats along the Pacific shore at twilight. Like a thousand mockingbirds all whistling and yodeling and singing in unison, or a flock of a million flamingos all taking flight at once!

And it will be powerful. Had you ever thought of that—that you will be powerful after you die? Perhaps this is the most incredible part of Paul's description. Traditionally, the grave has been thought of as a place where one has no power, where all strength has gone. But Paul says that the body that is raised up is powerful.

What is power, anyway? Is it the strength to bend others to our wills? Or is it being harmoniously connected with the Source of all being, so that the strength and vibrancy of the Source flow through us at all times, so that the power of the Source is in us?

In the film *Cocoon*, we were shown the widespread secular longing for bodies that are imperishable, glorious, and powerful. When the residents of a retirement village discover the secret of longevity and revitalization through some strange rocks possessed by interplanetary visitors, their bodies become powerful again. And when the alien beings invite the older folks to go with them to their planet and live forever, most of them elect to go; they want to be imperishable!

What was the film's special appeal to most of its audience, if not the desire for eternal life, often so denied by a secular society that it must sublimate its wishes in a whimsical story of this kind?

For the followers of Christ, such possibilities are not mere whimsy. Our faith is centered in a God who has the power to raise up our weak and perishable bodies after death and convert them into strong and everlasting bodies of a new kind, a heavenly kind, so that we may worship and glorify God forever. Our perishable natures will put on the imperishable, as Paul says, and our mortal natures will put on immortality (I Cor. 15:53). We shall become what it is in us now to become, but what we cannot become until we have died and the seed has been raised up by God into an incredible flowering!

Must we take it all on Paul's word, or is there corroboration from our own experience?

There are witnesses on almost every hand, if we will only notice them.

A woman in Los Angeles told me about the vision she had of her mother, who had been dead for more than thirty years. The woman was walking in a long hallway at her home, thinking of nothing in particular, when suddenly a circle of light about fifteen inches in diameter appeared near the baseboard ten or twelve feet ahead of her. It was an extremely bright light, divided equally into three segments—one gold, one rose, and the third bluish green. In the middle of the light, dressed in black, was the woman's mother.

"I remember she made that dress when she was about 60 years

old," said the woman, "and in this circle of light she looked 60, not 87, as she was when she died. She was looking directly at me, very serious and thoughtful."

The vision lasted several seconds. The woman was shocked and speechless, and afterward, told no one but family members about the incident. What seemed to astonish her most was her mother's youthfulness and vitality. The perishable body had put on the imperishable.

A woman in Texas lost her young son in a plane crash. Beyond the death itself, the thing that troubled her most was the fact that his face had been smashed and several teeth were missing.

"I cried all the time about it," she said, "imagining him going through eternity like that."

Then one night in a dream or a vision—she was not sure which—she saw him. His face was whole and his teeth were restored.

He smiled at her. "See, Mom, I'm all right. Don't worry about me."

The perishable had put on the imperishable.

Maurice Rawlings, a cardiovascular specialist in Chattanooga, Tennessee, was so impressed by his patients' glimpses of eternity in so-called life-after-life experiences that he kept records of them and has included some in his book *Beyond Death's Door*. One account is of a seventy-year-old man who had a heart attack and was rushed to the hospital. In the elevator of the hospital, he felt himself "die" and began an out-of-body experience in which he entered a doorway in a white wall and found himself in heaven—or at least on the outskirts of heaven. He saw a man clothed in a dazzling white robe, sitting and reading a large book.

"Are you Jesus?" he asked.

"No," said the man, "you will find Jesus and your loved ones beyond that door."

When the man went through the second door, he saw a beautiful, brilliantly lit city filled with golden domes and steeples. The streets were shining, not quite like marble but made of something he had never seen before. He saw many people clothed in white, all of them radiant and beautiful. The air was fresh and clean. He said he had never smelled anything like it. And there was beautiful music. His senses were totally involved.

Then he saw his mother and father, both of whom had died years before. His mother had been an amputee, but her leg was now restored.

He said to her, "You and Father are beautiful."

They said, "You have the same radiance, and you are also beautiful."

As they walked, they came to a building larger than all the others. It looked like a giant football stadium, with an open end from which emanated a light so bright that the man could not look at it. Many people seemed to be bowed in front of this building in adoration and prayer.

He said to his parents, "What is that?"

"In there is God," they answered.

The man had never seen anything like it. Everybody seemed to be happy. He had never felt such a sense of well-being. When the doctors brought him back to life, he was reluctant to come. He did not want to leave the great happiness he had found. But he knew he had to return and tell others about his experience. He said he would devote the remainder of his life to telling anyone who would listen.

Was the man hallucinating, or had he had a real foretaste of what it means for the perishable to put on the imperishable? His old body was nearly worn out. Was he anticipating what his new body would be like?

Paul himself had a vision in which he visited heaven. Maybe that is how he learned about the seed and the plant, the old body and the new body. It is all a mystery, he said. But it is somehow related to Christ and his resurrection. In this life we bear a strong resemblance to Adam, whose name meant "dust" or "earth"; in the life to come, we shall all resemble Christ. It is his spirit we shall share, his radiance, his glory, his power.

For the moment, we see only "puzzling reflections in a mirror," for our bodies are perishable, contemptible, and weak, and we are subject to great confusion. But when we have exchanged these earthly bodies for bodies that are imperishable, glorious, and powerful, we shall see "face to face," and everything will be clear (I Cor. 13:12). Now we have bodies for this season of life—bodies which serve us well enough for the seedtime. Then we shall have bodies for all seasons, bodies for eternity, and they will be beyond description!

. . . and the life everlasting.

THE LIFE
THAT NEVER ENDS

Robert Bolt's play *A Man for All Seasons* focuses on the life and death of Sir Thomas More, the stalwart humanist who refused to acknowledge Henry VIII as supreme head of the church in England and was beheaded for his obstinacy. In a moving and tender scene near the end of the play as More is conveyed to his execution, his daughter Margaret flings herself upon him, crying, "Father! Father! Father, Father, Father, Father!"—as if by pronouncing this filial noun she might absolve him of his political offense and bind him to this life.

"Have patience, Margaret," he says, "and trouble not thyself. Death comes for us all; even at our birth . . . death does but stand aside a little. And every day he looks towards us and muses somewhat to himself whether that day or the next he will draw nigh. It is the law of nature, and the will of God."

A few moments later he mounts the steps to the executioner's platform and turns to the headsman.

"Friend," he says, "be not afraid of your office. You send me to God."

Don't you wish you felt that certain about life after death? It would make dying much easier.

Why do you suppose we don't feel more certain?

Ours is a different age.

We live after Darwin and Marx and Freud.

We live after the Holocaust.

We live after Hiroshima.

We live in the nuclear era.

Our age is a product of science and technology.

Television manipulates our reality.

Most of us are not very certain about anything.

A recent national poll indicates that 94 percent of the American people believe in life after death—believe in it as an idea.

But having great personal confidence in it is another matter.

As John Updike says in his memoirs, *Self-Consciousness*, he learned even as a boy that most people don't really believe what they say they believe—even the pastors and elders of the church.

Most of us are terrified of death.

Like a young woman who had contracted AIDS from her ex-husband and was dying in the hospital. Her closest family members came to visit her. For two hours, they sat around talking while she brooded in silence.

Suddenly she burst out: "I wanna live! I wanna live!"

She brought her fist down on a chair repeatedly.

"I don't want to leave you!" she cried. "I don't want to leave my kids! I don't want to *leave! I bleepin' don't want to die!*"

We are afraid because we no longer live anticipating life after death. In Thomas More's time, people thought and talked about what it is like on the other side. In our time, we place primary emphasis on *this* life. We boogie all night and take drugs and drive fast cars, trying to crowd everything we can into the few years of consciousness we have, and we don't feel at all confident about what it will be like to die and move on.

We focus so intensely on this life that we lose touch with the next one.

Some people agonize about the loss of confidence.

Here are the words of Madison Scott, a psychiatrist in Dallas:

I want to live, personally, self-consciously, continuously, after death! Nothing less! Don't offer me anything less! I've tasted self-conscious existence. The fever is upon me. The passion is within me! And I do not apologize. I want life, more life—beyond death! If you can believe in death, final nothingness, then do it. I can't! I am alive, and I will not go gently into that good night. I will rage and rage against any and all reasonings, scientific or whatsoever, that logically insist that I am an organism, and, like all organisms, I am biodegradable in a city dump euphemistically called a cemetery. I do not intend to cease when the physiochemical processes stop. I can't help it—I will not help it! I have lived. I will not go serenely into oblivion! I listen to the incurable clamoring of my self-conscious self. I cannot and will not be bought off with consolation prizes like living on in posterity's memory. Posterity be hanged! We are talking about *my life*, my self-conscious, loving, laughing, confused, fallible, flourishing life! And when told I must prepare to die and rot into a compost pile, I am not neutral. I am not serene. I become obstreperous, clamorous, unruly! A thousand theories may be against me! I will listen to my *aliveness*, the steady experience of my self-consciousness! Out of the necessity of my self-conscious nature, I am desperate for life, now and forever! I make no apology! I want to live, and I can't help it. I don't want to help it. I want life, my life, my immortality.

Did you notice how many times the word *self-conscious* appeared in Dr. Scott's statement? That's the clue. We don't want to lose our consciousness of things. We want to go on living, being aware. We want the self to continue to have an existence as a center of knowledge and understanding.

The Apostle Paul understood the pain of this desire. "If our hope in Christ has been for this life only," he said, "we are of all people the most pitiable" (I Cor. 15:19 NJB).

When all is said and done, our faith in eternal life comes down to four things:

First, it depends upon our belief in God and the nature of God. If we believe God is love, then we must also believe that God has given us life for more than our time on earth. Otherwise, what could we say about those who spend most of their lives in pain and discomfort, or those who die before they have reached an age of understanding? What of those who have suffered unjustly or died on the battlefield with their promise unfulfilled? To believe in a

God of love is to believe in a life beyond this one, where hope and joy are complete and love has an opportunity to achieve its final fruition.

Second, it depends upon our faith in the witness of Christ. "I am the resurrection and the life," he said; "he who believes in me, though he die, yet shall he live, and whoever lives and believes in me shall never die" (John 11:25-26a). His other teachings are so credible; we have found them true as we have lived by them. Is there any reason to doubt that he understood about the afterlife as well?

Third, it depends upon what we know from the witness of church and society. What others believe and say is important to us. Sociologists speak of the social construction of reality—the part society plays in determining what is real for us. We tend to accept as true what many others say they believe. This becomes problematic in an age like ours, which is so highly secularized that many people do not openly express a belief in the supernatural or in a life after life. Even the church becomes reticent on such matters, not wishing to offend its friends in the general culture. It is important that such reticence be forsworn and that the church take as strong and courageous a stand as possible on the subject of eternal life, for if the salt has lost its power to season, then it is of no use.

Fourth, it depends upon our own understanding of the life to come, and upon the Spirit of God working in us to extend that understanding, to convince us of the absolute reality of that which we can neither see nor taste nor touch, but which we know of a certainty to exist. If we never think about life after death until we are confronted with death—our own or that of someone near to us—then of course we shall have no real faith in it. It should be a matter of frequent consideration and meditation, an object of our reading, a subject of our conversation. We should seek to understand it as we understand the nature of the physical universe or the workings of our own bodies. It is, after all, fully as important to our well-being as these other subjects.

What we believe about everlasting life greatly affects the way we live and how we feel about everything else.

Remember our friend the TV salesman and his formula for human behavior?

Behavior is determined by feelings.

Feelings are determined by attitudes.

Attitudes are determined by beliefs.

Beliefs are determined by programming.

If we pay constant attention to our input about the subject of life after death, counteracting the general tendency in today's society to neglect it, our belief in it will be strengthened. When this occurs, our attitudes and feelings about life will be changed in a positive way. The outcome will be the kind of behavior advocated by Jesus, in which we care more for the kingdom of God than for the perishable objects of this age; more for the welfare of other persons than for our own well-being.

Paul concluded his great peroration on eternal life in First Corinthians 15 with these words: "Therefore, my beloved brethren, be steadfast, immovable, always abounding in the work of the Lord, knowing that in the Lord your labor is not in vain" (vs. 58). He knew that there is a direct relationship between believing in the life to come and being steadfast, immovable, and abounding. When we know that this life is only the prelude to another and that the other is infinitely more beautiful and glorious than this one, it has a positive effect on everything we think or do. Making money and having a high time do not seem nearly so important then. What really matters is learning to live now with the grace and understanding of the life that awaits us!

How confidence in the life to come affects the way we live today is seen in the life of J. B. Phillips. While Phillips was serving as a young curate in Penge, outside of London, he nearly died of peritonitis. The surgeon who removed his appendix thought he wouldn't last through the night. He gave instructions to the nurse merely to make the patient as comfortable as possible. Toward morning, the restless young man had a dream about eternity:

I was alone, depressed and miserable, trudging wearily down a dusty slope. Around me were the wrecks and refuse of human living. There were ruined homes, pools of stagnant water, cast-off shoes, rusty tin cans, worn-out motor tyres and rubbish of every kind. Suddenly, as I picked my way amid this dreary mess, I looked up. Not far away, on the other side of a little valley, was a vista of indescribable beauty. (p. 73)

He gasped for breath at the loveliness of the pastoral scene. He saw mountains and streams, fields and forests, clouds and sky, and he heard birds singing everywhere.

Recognizing the scene as the home he had always sought, Phillips ran down the slope. As he neared the bottom, he spotted a shiny white bridge across the nearest stream and made for that. His heart was filled with joy at the thought of what he was about to experience.

But just as he reached the bridge, a figure in white appeared and, smiling gently, gestured for him to return up the dismal slope.

Never, he felt, had he known such bitter disappointment. But sadly he turned and began to retrace his steps. As he walked up the hill, he burst into tears.

At this, the dreamer awoke and found himself weeping.

The night nurse bent over him and said soothingly, "What are you crying for? You've come through tonight—now you're going to live!"

"My heart was too full of the vision," wrote Phillips, "for me to make any reply; what could I say to someone who had not seen what I had seen?"

All his life, Phillips remembered this vivid dream. In his final months of life, he said that "it remains as true and clear to me today as it was then."

It was out of his abiding certainty of the life to come—the life he had almost entered that night—that J. B. Phillips drew the strength and inspiration to carry on his formidable work as a translator and witness to the gospel, traveling around the globe and bringing hope and courage to millions. He was not immune to the normal pressures and vicissitudes of life. On the contrary, he went through a period in which he was sadly and deeply depressed; he described those agonies in his autobiography. During the most severe part of the depression, he says, he lost emotional touch with God, but he never lost his faith. And finally, when he once more made his way down that dusty slope to the shining white bridge across the stream—this time to cross the bridge and enter the paradise he had seen so many years before—he departed this life with a quiet confidence, a confidence he had carried undiminished in his heart since that restless night in the hospital.

There could be no more fitting words to conclude this book than those with which Phillips closed his autobiography, *The Price of Success*:

In my opinion whatever we may have to go through now is less than nothing compared with the magnificent future God has in store for us. The whole creation is on tiptoe to see the wonderful sight of the sons of God coming into their own. The world of creation cannot see as yet reality, not because it chooses to be blind, but because in God's purpose it has been so limited—yet it has been given hope. And the hope is that in the end the whole of created life will be rescued from the tyranny of change and decay, and have its share in that magnificent liberty which can only belong to the children of God! (p. 215)